"The path to success full of myths and legends. Nenad Pacek gives a truly insightful, practical and colorful perspective of the rabbit hole. This will be the road book for many international executives!"

– Ümit Subasi
Member of the Executive Board and head of
Latin America, CIS, Middle East and Africa, Beiersdorf

"A must read book for executives who want to know what it takes to outperform competitors on a sustainable basis in emerging markets. The insights are highly valuable."

– Chris Zanetti
Regional Vice President, EMEA
Merck Consumer Health Care

"Nenad shares his wealth of experience in emerging markets in a concise and digestible manner for the busy executive. He has collected not only his own experiences, but draws on the best practice from the numerous companies with which he consults. This book is a must read for anyone trying to make sense of business and economics in today's dynamic and turbulent markets."

– Ian Hudson
President, EMEA, DuPont

"As always, Nenad is stimulating and challenging. Are we up to the challenge?"

– John Langdell
Vice President, Business Development
International Markets, SC Johnson

"This is a great read for anyone concerned with future business growth. The recommended concepts are to the point, practical in nature and therefore easy to apply in a real market and organizational context. Nenad's advice is built on solid foundations of thorough analysis of fundamental business drivers and consulting work with a large number of multinational companies."

– Jan Hillered, Senior Vice President,
Europe and CIS, Western Union

"A must read for Global Business Leaders... Nenad Pacek brilliantly combines the understanding of global macro trends, with real life business knowledge. This is what makes his work so valuable."

– Vladimir Makatsaria,
President EMEA, Johnson & Johnson Medical

Nenad Pacek's extraordinary new book will serve as both a tremendous resource and insightful guide in the coming decade for business leaders at all levels who want to build and sustain their business in the emerging markets. A must read!

– John Ryan
CEO, Center for Creative Leadership

THE FUTURE OF BUSINESS IN EMERGING MARKETS

Brent,

Hats off to you for navigating through a very challenging project!

Heres to the future & the legacy we leave behind from the 4.0 journey.

Kevin Isaac
DECEMBER 2012

NENAD PACEK

THE FUTURE OF BUSINESS IN EMERGING MARKETS

GROWTH STRATEGIES FOR GROWTH MARKETS

Copyright © 2012 Nenad Pacek
Published by Marshall Cavendish Business
An imprint of Marshall Cavendish International

1 New Industrial Road, Singapore 536196
genrefsales@sg.marshallcavendish.com
www.marshallcavendish.com/genref

Marshall Cavendish is a trademark of Times Publishing Limited

Other Marshall Cavendish offices:
Marshall Cavendish Corporation. 99 White Plains Road, Tarrytown NY 10591–9001, USA • Marshall Cavendish International (Thailand) Co Ltd. 253 Asoke, 12th Floor, Sukhumvit 21 Road, Klongtoey Nua, Wattana, Bangkok 10110, Thailand • Marshall Cavendish (Malaysia) Sdn Bhd, Times Subang, Lot 46, Subang Hi-Tech Industrial Park, Batu Tiga, 40000 Shah Alam, Selangor Darul Ehsan, Malaysia

The right of Nenad Pacek to be identified as the author of this work has been asserted by him in accordance with the Copyright, Designs and Patents Act 1988.

All rights reserved

No part of this publication may be reproduced, stored in a retrieval system or transmitted, in any form or by any means, electronic, mechanical, photocopying, recording or otherwise, without the prior permission of the copyright owner. Requests for permission should be addressed to the publisher.

The authors and publisher have used their best efforts in preparing this book and disclaim liability arising directly and indirectly from the use and application of this book. All reasonable efforts have been made to obtain necessary copyright permissions. Any omissions or errors are unintentional and will, if brought to the attention of the publisher, be corrected in future printings.

A CIP record for this book is available from the British Library

ISBN 978-981-4346-31-3

Cover design by Cover Kitchen

Printed and bound by CPI Group (UK) Ltd, Croydon, CR0 4YY

CONTENTS

Author's preface   9

Introduction   16

CHAPTER 1   18
Economic Mega-trends until 2020

CHAPTER 2   41
Strategic and Structural Success Factors

CHAPTER 3   104
Building and Executing Marketing Excellence

CHAPTER 4   144
Human Resources Wisdom for the Future

CHAPTER 5   177
Acquisitions as a Way to Grow

CHAPTER 6   201
Tips for Executive Survival and Advancement in Emerging Markets

CHAPTER 7   211
Best Practices for Medium-sized Firms Going Regional or Global

CHAPTER 8   218
Strategic and Business Economic Outlooks by Region

CHAPTER 9   245
Selected Economic Risks Executives Should be Aware of

Epilogue   261

Bibliography   265

About the Author   268

AUTHOR'S PREFACE

THIS BOOK IS ABOUT TWO THINGS. First, it focuses on what companies must do today in order to be successful in emerging markets in the future. Second, it helps executives understand outlooks for various parts of the world. In its predominant business part, it focuses only on those things that I concluded were the most relevant after talking to countless executives and observing many firms over the last few years. This is not an international business textbook. It is a more advanced text, focusing only on critical success factors for the future. It has been written for those who wish to accelerate sales growth in emerging markets in a sustainable way and for those who wish to build strong market positions. This is not a scientific work and does not pretend to be, although it does use some good practices for writing qualitative scientific papers – before I labeled something a trend, there needed to be a critical mass of corporate opinion and/or actions underpinning it. The book is mostly about business practice, although in the first and last chapters I also put my international economist hat on to explain economic megatrends and medium-term strategic economic outlooks for key regions and countries.

This book has been written for executives at global, regional and country management level of sizeable international companies (and those that wish to become more international), but it will also be hugely beneficial for those executives who run international business for medium-sized firms who see stronger international business as a way to survive. One section of the book specifically addresses several key issues for medium-sized firms.

These opening words were the last I wrote for this book. I wrote the preface on a flight from Dubai to Vienna, my home base for over 20 years, considering why it took me over two years to write this relatively concise book.

The first reason for taking so long to complete the book is that I wanted to talk to, and observe, many senior regional and global executives operating in different sectors and find out how their strategies for international markets were changing, or in which direction they wanted them to change, in order to ensure lasting success in emerging markets. I was adamant that the core of the book had to be about corporate practice by people who have seen it all and whose livelihoods depend on finding sales growth in emerging markets. And I wanted enough executives to confirm certain trends that I had encountered during numerous advisory sessions. In other words, there had to be a critical mass of opinion or action before something became a visible trend.

Secondly, I wanted to use the input from in-house strategic planning corporate sessions, where I so often speak, advise and listen to multinationals as they plan for the future. Inputs from such in-house and client group sessions of the CEEMEA Business Group added another dimension to the individual views of executives.

Third, I wanted to have time to internalize what I'd heard and let various trends sit in my mind for some time so that I could start adding personal dimensions and opinions as well as group the trends when they were ready to be put on paper. In other words, this book was being written even when I was not actually writing it. I wanted also to see how some of the new trends gelled with past lessons learned, which I described in my book, *Emerging Markets: Lessons for Business Success and Outlook for Different Markets,* in 2007.

And fourth, I just did not have enough time to write it quickly! As a result, this book was almost entirely written in three locations: aircraft, airport lounges and my home office, usually between 4 and 6 a.m., when my wife and two daughters were still fast asleep. They say that Stephen King wrote most of his horror stories starting at 4 a.m. In many firms, emerging markets expansion is actually beginning to look like a horror story, as executives are being asked to deliver more without the necessary resources!

This book is about preventing such horror stories from developing; it is about shedding light on the new complexities of international business; and it is ultimately about how to succeed in that complex emerging markets environment in the future.

I divided the book into several sections that describe what companies need to do today to ensure they outperform competition in emerging markets in a sustainable way: economic and business megatrends in the external environment; strategic and structural foundations for long-lasting success; marketing excellence issues; human resources issues; acquisitions as a way to grow a business; tips for executive survival and advancement; best practices for medium sized firms; and strategic economic outlooks for regions and selected markets.

I would like to thank all my clients who keep using my personal advice on business trends and markets – those who continue to use my company Global Success Advisors and CEEMEA Business Group corporate service to build, change or fine-tune their international strategies and to keep up-to-date with developments in markets around the world. Without executives' generous input this book would not exist and this book is dedicated to the thousands of decent, smart, hard-working executives whom I have had the privilege to meet and interact with over the last two decades. And because this book is written for very busy executives who have no time to read and who must find growth every year, it is both very concise and focused predominantly on the most important current and future corporate practices, rather than theories (or descriptions of how to open a letter of credit!).

I bring to this book a mix of professional experiences that marry the world of business, economics and management:

- In my day-to-day work I advise global and regional management of international companies on economic outlooks of all regions and almost all countries in the world.

- I have managed regional and global businesses and got my hands "dirty" in some of the toughest emerging markets (particularly in Eastern Europe, the Middle East and Africa).
- I have been observing and proactively researching corporate best practices for international expansion for almost 20 years and they were described in my previous two books on emerging markets. This served as a great foundation for this look into the future.
- I have travelled to 90-plus countries (and counting) on business and chaired business events with over a hundred prime ministers or presidents (some of whom, by the way, were knowledgeable and brilliant and some of whom knew about economics or business as little as my plumber).
- Through my business advisory work and public speaking at large and small corporate events, I meet hundreds of senior executives every year who run corporate or entrepreneurial activities in the international business arena. Their tremendous business insights are partly woven into this book.

You will notice that I exchange my business and economic hats throughout this book and my hope is that you will find this useful and interesting. I aim to make this book full of "must know" stuff rather than "nice to know".

My special thanks goes to my wife Antonija and my older daughter Nina for patiently waiting while I work and travel to all corners of the world. They understand that economic and business issues in emerging markets are my long-standing and ongoing intellectual passion, and I am deeply grateful to them. My younger daughter

Alina is still too young to understand what Daddy does and by the time she understands, I promised to my family that I will finally slow down. I also dedicate this book to my third daughter who is coming into the world in July 2012.

I hope you will find this book useful. Please feel free to contact me at *nenad.pacek@globalsuccessadvisors.eu*.

Nenad Pacek
Austria, March 2012

INTRODUCTION

One's first step to wisdom is to question everything – and one's last is to come to terms with everything.

—*Georg Christoph Lichtenberg*

GROWTH IS A BUSINESS obsession and always will be. But achieving sustainable, profitable growth in emerging markets has been a difficult and hugely underestimated exercise for most companies. During the last few years, it has become obvious that succeeding in emerging markets is more complicated than ever. I am deeply convinced that it will get even more complicated with every year that goes by. Unprecedented changes in the competition landscape as well as economic vulnerabilities of the global economy are just two underlying external reasons for this increasing complexity.

While this book partly looks at external changes that impact companies operating in emerging markets, its main goal is to examine what companies should be doing now to be successful in emerging markets in the next decade and beyond.

When I started to write the first edition of *Emerging Markets: Lessons for Business Success and Outlook for Different Markets* back in early 2003, the world was in so many ways different from today. Back then, even half-hearted international business strategies somehow worked – at least for a while. In the book's second edition I focused on why companies failed in the past in emerging markets (and many of those lessons are still important bedrocks for any emerging market strategy). This book partly revisits and re-examines some of those business lessons, but it is primarily about the future.

Having a strong emerging markets business is not only about growth, but about long-term corporate survival. It is now very clear that most parts of the developed world will be sub-par growth areas in the future. Growth will mainly come from emerging markets. Any executive and company in search of international business growth today will have to rethink everything about how to do international business – and pay attention to more internal and external issues than ever before. The pace of change in the external environment often exceeds the pace of change within companies, and for many companies this will lead to a growing number of problems – unless these are addressed with speed, urgency and smart strategies. I will address these issues in this book.

Before I examine how companies should approach the next decade and beyond in international and emerging markets, let's look first at three key economic megatrends that will shape the world during the next decade.

Chapter 1

ECONOMIC MEGA-TRENDS UNTIL 2020

Today you can go to a gas station and find the cash register open and the toilets locked. They must reckon toilet paper is worth more than money.

—*Joey Bishop*

IN THIS CHAPTER I WILL highlight three economic mega trends that demonstrate why it is important for companies to increase their corporate focus, attention and investment on emerging markets. These three trends can be broken down thus:
- An age of moderate and highly volatile global growth
- The poor medium-term outlook for the developed world
- The continued economic rise of emerging markets

1. AN AGE OF MODERATE AND HIGHLY VOLATILE GLOBAL GROWTH

We have had more economic crises in the last 35 years than in the previous 350 years (see Kindleberger). There are quite a few things that have contributed to this unusual volatility and the recent big global crisis (from which we still have not really recovered). In the last decades we have been living in an age of massive deregulation, primarily of financial markets. Things such as the "securitization" of risk; free flows of often speculative capital to currencies, commodities and other asset classes; liberalization of short-term capital flows, even for the poorest markets; the rise of financial instruments that few authorities understand; selling of so called Triple-A rated securities to unsuspecting buyers; and massaging balance sheets to hide liabilities in some banks and shadow banks, have all contributed to the currently messy and worrying economic environment.

The rise of the largest global credit bubble ever was the pinnacle of the credit party built on easy money, easy liquidity and allegedly financial fraud, crime and corruption (just think about how the global credit bubble was created prior to 2008). The credit party ended with a mega crisis from which many areas of the world are still trying to recover. And the recovery will take a long time. (I discuss the problems and possible solutions for the world economy in my latest executive handbook, *Global Economy*, published by Marshall Cavendish in July 2012).

The good news is that another 1930s-style Great Depression was avoided, despite the fact that this latest crisis was about four times larger than the Great Depression as a percentage of global GDP. It was avoided because the *initial* policy response was broadly good in many countries, even if often coming too late (because authorities did not really know what kind of financial monster was actually coming over the horizon). Monetary stimulus, fiscal stimulus, recapitalization of banks, injections of liquidity into the banks, rescuing banks from collapse, buying up toxic assets and even printing money in many countries (these days popularly called "quantitative easing") all played a role in preventing a total collapse.

Despite these measures, however, we still ended up in the Great Recession of the late 2000s. The reasons were that the sheer size, speed and complexity of the crisis caused enough delays in official responses that it shattered private and corporate confidence. The result was like a massive earthquake – today, we live in the world of aftershocks. These will not stop any time soon.

Economic history tells us that once private and corporate confidence is shattered, it always takes a long time to rebuild. This is particularly the case in crises that have financial and banking problems as their root cause.

Some markets are already recovering reasonably well, while others will take longer to recover. The speed of recovery in the short and medium term will partly depend on their accumulated debt. More debts equals higher deleveraging need, and that equals lower growth and weaker business prospects. Today, the developed world holds significantly more debts in absolute and percentage terms than emerging markets. The developed world will be going through the process of extended deleveraging for years to come. And because the European Union, the United States and Japan still represent the majority (over 60%) of world output (measured at market exchange rates), inevitably this will keep *overall* global growth more moderate. We have therefore entered the age of a more moderate and more volatile economic growth globally. Some call it a new normal. The truth is that a few years prior to the global crisis (think of the economic

> **The truth is that a few years prior to the global crisis (think of the economic and business boom in 2006 and 2007), we were living in the "new abnormal", which was not sustainable.**

and business boom in 2006 and 2007), we were living in the "new abnormal", which was not sustainable.

Why will global growth struggle in the medium term? Many of the points below refer to the developed world.

a) The massive age of leverage enjoyed by businesses will not return for decades, even if regulators do a half-hearted job (which they will inevitably do). Although the financial industry is known for its creativity, it will be hard to hide, package or sell liabilities to third parties as long as memories of selling the so-called Triple-A rated securities to unsuspecting buyers do not fade away. And without hiding, packaging and selling liabilities, it will be hard to build another massive credit bubble. Therefore, growth will not reach the super cyclical peak it reached in 2006 and 2007, perhaps for decades. Current extra liquidity pumped by central banks, which is producing current growth in the US for example, will also not last forever.

b) The need to restore balance sheets at government, household and private levels will continue, particularly in the developed world and some emerging markets (mostly in Central and Eastern Europe).

c) Unemployment historically rises for at least four years from the beginning of any financially-induced crisis (see Rogoff and Reinhart). In developed markets, particularly the European Union, the gradual recovery will be largely jobless for several years. This means that the consumer will remain psychologically fragile, reducing their level of spending. And if private spending is weak, GDP growth can't boom either.

d) Lending will remain tight and subdued for many years, particularly for smaller and medium-sized firms. There are a number of reasons why banks will continue to operate in the so-called "reduced risk mode" over the next few years: new regulations (also a new recapitalization drive in the Eurozone) are forcing them to increase their capital ratios. More cash hoarding is likely, non-performing loans are high in many countries, and some banks still need to clean "toxic waste" (previously known as Triple-A rated securities) from their balance sheets.

e) Previous crises show that memories of the crisis linger on for many years in private and corporate minds. Exuberant confidence is unlikely to return for years after the end of the actual crisis. Cautiousness predominates. No one should underestimate the importance of psychology in post-crisis environments.

f) High and rising government debt in the developed world and pressures on government budgets in other regions (due to falling tax revenues, and to a lesser extent, stimulus measures) mean that governments will be seeking to live much closer within their means. To achieve this, governments might introduce tax rises and/or various spending cuts. And austerity, even if moderate, means less growth in the near future. Sadly, most developed countries today talk about austerity, and then some more austerity. This "austerity philosophy" comes at a time when private and corporate confidence is still fragile, especially in the developed world. What the world actually needs in the short term is more fiscal stimulus to grow again. Sadly, this important lesson from history is often forgotten or ignored.

g) Even emerging markets will grow more slowly than in the past as buyers from the developed world buy fewer exports from these emerging markets. But the important thing for executives and companies to remember is that emerging markets will outperform the developed world for years to come in terms of economic and sales growth (see the third economic trend below). Today, it is the developed world that has high debts and low reserves and it is emerging markets that have low debt levels and high reserves.

2. THE POOR MEDIUM-TERM OUTLOOK FOR THE DEVELOPED WORLD

The underlying reasons for the poor economic outlook in the US, the Eurozone and Japan are already partly described above. Below, I offer a more detailed analysis.

THE EUROZONE

Only two large, strategic markets in the Western European part of the Eurozone do not have too high a public debt: Luxembourg and Finland. All others are above the broadly accepted international benchmark of 60% of GDP. On aggregate, gross government debt in the Eurozone was, in early 2012, estimated at 91% of GDP, and rising.

Countries usually have five choices in how to reduce public debt burdens to more sustainable levels.
- First, they can default on their payments.
- Second, they can run a high inflation rate, hoping this will eat away their debts.

- Third, they can increase tax rates.
- Fourth, they can cut spending.
- Fifth, they can accelerate growth through fiscal and monetary stimulus and seek to grow out of their debt problem.

The most likely scenario for indebted Western European markets is that they will take the third and fourth options in combination. And in many countries this is already happening. The latest documents released by the EU (following a recent endless series of summits on how to resolve the euro crisis), all praise austerity as a way forward. Don't get me wrong, I have nothing against spending only what you earn and maintaining low debts. But austerity is the wrong approach when private and corporate confidence is not there. Even the International Monetary Fund (IMF) recently published a paper saying that austerity does not really produce growth in the short term. Economic history teaches us that countries that do austerity during tough economic times usually experience a prolonged period of no or slow growth and lower purchasing power at every level in their economy.

This is bad news for business in the Eurozone in the next three to five years. Those economies that are globally competitive (i.e., those that joined the euro first) will do better than others, since their export engines will continue to help. There is also a broad, corporate consensus among my clients that says, "We will not see much sales growth in the Eurozone in the next few years." In the Eurozone, the next years will be a perpetual struggle to save the euro.

So how did the Eurozone, one of the pillars of the global economy, end up in need of deleveraging? First, most markets in the Eurozone went into the global crisis with decent fundamentals and public debt was mostly at acceptable levels, except in places like Greece and Italy. But as the crisis evolved public debt burdens rose quickly for two reasons. On the one hand, some of the banks' losses were taken over by governments. The authorities saw it as paramount to rescue banks but they had to nationalize debts in the process (the poor tax payers will have to pay for these debts for years to come). Also, as most EU economies went into recession in 2009, tax revenues fell, putting further pressure on public debt. Also, many markets in the Eurozone periphery accumulated large foreign debts (which included household and corporate debt because interest rates were low), but this went unnoticed, since they were part of the Eurozone (more on this later).

Sovereign debt crisis

But an even bigger issue for the Eurozone in the short term is the sovereign debt crisis, which is constantly threatening to infect the entire area. To explain the sovereign debt crisis and its principal sources, we need to take a step back. This will also help us understand how the crisis might play out in the future and what the impact on business could be.

Was the introduction of the common currency, the euro, a wise idea in the first place from an economic standpoint? Before the introduction of the euro, many academics in respected economic journals wrote that the euro did not make sense because you could never have one interest rate for such a diverse group of markets, growing at different paces. Many academics argued that you could run a single currency, the dollar, for 50 US states because when someone loses a job, he can pack his bags and drive around the country looking for work elsewhere. In Europe, it is much less likely that the Greeks or the Portuguese will quickly pack their bags and go and work in Finland. We could see throughout the existence of the euro that interest rates for some countries were too low (creating housing bubbles in Spain and Ireland) and for some others they were too high.

It is a myth that all the blame for the Eurozone sovereign debt crisis lies in the peripheral countries, such as Greece and Portugal. The story is a bit more complex.

- Firstly, all Eurozone countries, except Luxembourg and Finland, hold larger-than-benchmark public debt.
- Secondly, when times were good, the European Central Bank (ECB) allowed all member states (despite the size of their current account deficit or foreign debt, which in some locations was completely out of control) to have equal access to its discount window.
- Third, banks treated sovereign debt from all member states equally and bought debt indiscriminately. This unnatural demand, needless to say, pushed interest rates down in countries that did not deserve low interest rates. The result was an explosion of credit and multiple housing bubbles, from which markets like Ireland and Spain are still recovering.
- Fourth, if any of the high current account deficit markets and high foreign debt markets (such as Spain or Ireland) had been outside of the Eurozone, they would have started raising

questions from creditors much earlier. Within the Eurozone this was not recognized, and good old macroeconomic principles were simply thrown out of the window.
- Fifth, what was the reason to push economies that were clearly not ready for the euro to still join the Eurozone? There are a bunch of conspiracy theories out there, involving financial and industrial lobbies (just check them out on the internet).
- Sixth, why did everybody ignore the obvious statistical games played in Athens, and perhaps in a few other markets, which involved cutting corners to meet the financial criteria for joining the euro?
- Seventh, why did credit rating agencies not sound the alarm in markets where foreign debt was becoming unsustainable? Too many questions still linger and economic researchers will argue the case for years to come.

Or course, some of the southern European markets (notably Greece) did massage their government accounting in order to join the Eurozone. They had an incentive to do so, since interest rates in their countries came down quickly after the introduction of the euro. But they cannot shoulder all the blame, since the story started earlier and was part of the grand political project to ultimately create a strong political union in Europe.

Perhaps the most disturbing aspect of the whole sovereign debt crisis is the reaction of the various authorities. In all aspects of their response – content, speed and approach – European governments could have done much better, much sooner. The fact that Greek debt is now seen as riskier than Venezuela is embarrassing for

Europe and a big proof that Europe's response at least partially failed. After such an embarrassment, the markets are now, unsurprisingly, beginning to question the entire Eurozone project, as well as the political integrity of the European Union.

When rumours of the Greek crisis first appeared, like many other observers, I expected the big political and economic family that is the European Union to quickly and discreetly help its family member in trouble. It was reasonable to expect that the EU would quietly meet the Greek leadership, provide all necessary cash and liquidity, and in return ask for a *very gradual* restructuring of its flawed fiscal and economic policy. I did not expect the Greek case to continue to make headline news.

So why did the Greek debt crisis develop and why we are now talking about further contagion in other markets? When they asked some of the key EU leaders what they would do about Greece, the response was something like, "We are still thinking about it". It was the same response for weeks, then months. The procrastination of response and insistence on deep austerity (we know that deep and hasty austerity measures kill growth and increase public debt) in return for a bailout all encouraged the fear of contagion. The German chancellor and her minister of finance even suggested that a country could leave the euro or even be expelled. Needless to say, the markets went crazy and demanded even bigger premiums on Greek debt, but also on debt generated by many other EU countries.

The conditions forced on Greece are impossible to implement and do remind me of the IMF's conditions imposed on Asian markets after the 1997 financial crisis. Those conditions made the crisis worse in the countries that took the advice, compared to those markets that ignored IMF strictures. This was scientifically demonstrated by Dani Rodrik at Harvard University (I wrote about this in 2003 in *Emerging Markets*). And yet Germany and other big countries in the EU imposed on Greece a rapid and deep austerity that guarantees recession will linger for a long time and that Greece has no chance of reducing its debts in the foreseeable future (even with the latest haircut and a bailout package).

The imposed austerity program, with its extraordinary speed and depth, ignores many hard-learned lessons of economic history. One of those is that public debt rises after a crisis largely due to lower tax revenues, rather than any impact of fiscal stimulus. The second is that deep and fast austerity makes recessions worse and does not really help reduce public debt. Third, fiscal austerity, as recent evidence from the IMF suggests, does not boost short-term economic growth and confidence (in contrast to what the ECB and other EU authorities are telling us).

Outlook for Western Europe

So what next for Western Europe? Western European markets outside the Eurozone are in relatively good economic shape. Norway, with its oil reserves, and competitive and low-debt Sweden, Denmark and Switzerland will all do better than the majority of Eurozone markets in the next three to five years, and possibly longer. Those countries within the Eurozone that are globally competitive and have something to sell to the rest of the world (particularly to fast-growing emerging markets), will manage to reduce their public debts sooner than those markets whose global competitiveness is weak. Markets that belong to this group include Finland, Austria, Germany (because of its export engine), parts of France, northern Italy and the parts of Dutch industry that are export-oriented.

The toughest outlook is for Greece, followed by Portugal, Ireland and Spain. Belgium, with its public debt of over 100% of GDP and political volatility, will make some serious fiscal adjustment in the next years, which in turn will hurt growth. Deep austerity measures in the United Kingdom will hurt its growth for several years (although the UK government, like the US, is lucky to have a pragmatic central bank that buys government bonds during the crisis and is therefore able to finance itself cheaply). Remember that such monetization of debt is essentially printing money; this approach does not cause inflation rates to rise as long as private and corporate confidence is low, and as long as it does not go on for too long.

Sadly, the European Central Bank has a narrow mandate of focusing on the inflation rate only. The downside of the whole euro story is the fact that countries in the euro club have lost their monetary sovereignty. It would be much easier for Italy or Spain to be able to cover part of their budget deficits and borrowing needs through Italian and Spanish central banks buying new government bonds directly (just like the US and British governments are doing now). This would not cost anything and it would not cause the inflation rate to rise, since domestic confidence is low; instead of borrowing at rates of 7% plus, countries would be able to borrow at almost no cost.

But we are not there. Conspiracy theorists nowadays argue that the euro project is just a long-standing plot concocted by powerful private financial institutions who own the US Federal Reserve to eliminate the ability of EU governments to control their own monetary destiny, and instead have them rely on expensive loans (lending to governments has been a big business for centuries). If this conspiracy theory is even partly correct, then the Eurozone will be rescued one way or the other, because the last thing the private lenders would want is to have various governments in the EU control their ability to print money again. I do not comment on conspiracy theories. The intelligent reader can make up his or her own mind. The truth is that various European governments would, indeed, benefit from an ability to control their own monetary destiny – just like the British, US and so many others in the world already do.

Public debt reductions in the Eurozone are likely to be borne by tax payers. This means weak private confidence, which will continue to affect corporate confidence, leading to weak demand and low growth for years to come. Companies selling to exporters that are strong in emerging markets and those selling things that improve corporate efficiency will do better than others.

The risk still remains of the sovereign debt contagion to Spain and Italy forming the next phase. This would kill the slowly recovering banking sectors in creditor markets considering hundreds of billions of dollars of sovereign debt held by EU banks. So far the strategy of the EU authorities has been to do just enough and to avert the big debt crisis at the last minute. With Mario Draghi at the helm of the European Central Bank, the monetary policy got more proactive in early 2012. Its last provision of 1 trillion euros to banks at 1% can in part be seen as "money printing through the back door". It surely prevented a major credit crunch and global meltdown in early 2012. During the political muddle-through-the-crisis type of approach, perhaps the biggest political damage to the whole European project is in undermining trust and confidence among EU countries.

I am a big fan of modern Western Europe (it is probably the most civilized place to live on the planet in human history) and the historic European Union project, and it is a shame that short-sightedness and ideology have now contributed to this serious deterioration of the political, economic and social foundations of the European Union. Further deterioration should not be allowed if the EU project is to thrive over the medium and long term. It would indeed be a great shame if the great goals of the EU, which are supposed to bring long-term political stability to a region ravaged by centuries of war, start to fall apart because of the inability to deal with the sovereign debt crisis. Worse, to fall apart over an economically stupid idea, such as the euro (which was introduced prematurely in too many countries, too quickly).

When some European leaders recently said, "If the euro fails, so will the EU", I was a bit surprised. The European Union project was doing well without the euro. It is the euro that is causing the current political problems in the EU, and the sooner governments realize that the monetary flexibility of member countries is important, the better it will be for the European Union as a whole. I am not sure the euro can exist unless serious fiscal union is in place and current policy goes in that direction. But I do question the sustainability of such a fiscal union (or even political union that many politicians are keen on), since it largely represents the end of country-level monetary/fiscal independence and democracy.

EU responses

So what is the EU doing now to contain this crisis, but more importantly, to create a system that will prevent future crises of this kind? The European Central Bank initially reacted reasonably well to the crisis, providing liquidity to the banking sector, which kept interest rates low. (This provision of liquidity increased under the new governor in 2012.) This probably saved Europe from going into another Great Depression and it is crucially important for the underlying stability of banks.

It is the euro that is causing the current political problems in the EU, and the sooner governments realize that the monetary flexibility of member countries is important, the better it will be for the European Union as a whole.

In recent months, the ECB even started to do something it was not supposed to do – print money, but only in minimal amounts compared to the US and UK governments. When some of the peripheral markets could not raise financing in international markets and there was the threat of further contagion, the ECB stepped in and bought government bonds. This is called "monetizing", and it is very similar to printing money. At the time of writing, the total amount that was "printed" was less than €200 billion. Compared to over US $3 trillion of quantitative easing in the US and some 1 trillion pounds in the UK, European monetary stimulus was minimal and reactive. And it was done out of fear of sovereign debt contagion bankrupting Western European banks. So the ECB chose the lesser of two evils. But it is clear that the ECB does not want to continue with the practice of buying government bonds and is putting the burden of a solution back to member governments.

The latest talk is about more economic integration through closer fiscal union. If the idea is to rescue the euro, fiscal union is a good solution, because no monetary union has ever survived without fiscal union. But I worry that this will push the European Union into even greater political problems. Why? Because fiscal union will be impossible to implement without deeper political union, and this is where troubles could intensify. It would be better to keep the Eurozone for a smaller group of countries that are globally competitive, that can thrive with a fixed exchange rate and that have converged gradually since the end of World War II. The others would benefit from more monetary flexibility in the next decade or two until they become more competitive, and until they converge with more advanced countries in the EU.

Is it possible that some countries will leave the euro, and how would this work in practice?

Economic history is full of examples of monetary unions breaking up (Scandinavia, the Latin monetary union). It is perfectly possible that this one will break up too down the road, with some serious disruption for business in the short term. In the old days, when each EU country had their own currency, markets like Italy or Greece would devalue their currencies as a way to keep exports competitive and to correct economic imbalances that could lead to bigger debt problems. They would also print more money during downturns to pay the wages of public servants, such as teachers and police officers. With the euro's fixed exchange rate and lack of monetary flexibility, any adjustment goes into the real economy in the form of lower wages and the overall shrinking of economic activity.

The simple truth is that the austerity measures are too harsh for markets such as Greece or Portugal. It could well be that ordinary people in these countries will simple say "this is unbearable", and will continue to protest and riot, triggering mega political crises. This could then lead to their governments deciding to abandon the Eurozone. Although various EU treaties stipulate that a country cannot leave the EMU, if a sovereign government decides to do so, it is hard to see what could stop them. In any case, any country that decided to leave the euro would face tremendous short term technical difficulties, such as the cost of printing and minting new currency, handling euro-denominated liabilities (a country would probably have to introduce an interim fixed rate with the euro in order to keep markets relatively calm), and the problem of how to prevent local savers from withdrawing deposits *en masse*. The bottom line for business is that there is a real possibility that some countries might seek to leave the Eurozone in the next few years, and in such countries there would be major economic disruption in the short term (but over the medium to long term they would benefit from newly-found monetary sovereignty).

UNITED STATES

Despite recent stock market jumps and some business recovery due to fiscal and monetary easing, most senior executives these days will readily admit that it will be hard to grow their business in the

US in the near future, unless a company very frequently comes up with incredibly innovative, exciting products or creates products for cheaper market segments. The broad corporate consensus about the US is that it will be hard to rely on pure economic growth to drive business forward in the foreseeable future.

The US economy was deeply affected during the Great Recession, with output shrinking 2.6% in 2009. While the United States is recovering, the bad news for business is that unemployment is still too high. Private and corporate confidence in the US economy is still shaky. Like in Europe, multinational companies are sitting on record amounts of cash and are not reinvesting enough. Consumers are still indebted and house prices are still flat. Even the US Federal Reserve recently said that it was not clear if a US recovery could be self sustained once the effects of a sizeable fiscal stimulus, and even bigger monetary stimulus, fade away during 2012–13.

One of the underlying problems in the US is the sizeable accumulation of gross government debt. At some 100% of GDP, it is even worse than the Eurozone. The worrying thing is the upward trend – the IMF estimates that the debt will rise to 112% by 2016. The budget deficit is among the highest in the world, at over 10% of GDP. Like in Europe, the US will probably introduce some austerity measures, especially if the Republicans take over the presidency in 2013.

Things could have been worse. In the first months of the global crisis, all US indicators were basically mirroring the beginning of the Great Depression of 1929. But the reaction to the crisis, although somewhat delayed, was broadly better than in Europe. Fiscal stimulus was larger and in particular, the Federal Reserve carried out a long list of unprecedented and unorthodox measures to revive growth. At over US $3 trillion, monetary stimulus, which is still ongoing in the latest incarnation called "The Twist", was immense. Because of all these measures, the US economy bounced back in 2010 and continued growing in 2011.

However, growth is almost certainly going to be much less than the pre-crisis period for years to come. Fiscal austerity, eventual withdrawal of quantitative easing, eventual increase in interest rates and still stubborn unemployment will all have an impact on growth and corporate sales in the foreseeable future. Questions are also being posed by credit rating agencies about the sustainability of the US debt position, something that was unthinkable just a few years ago. The crisis, as well as economic policies that have been for years remote from the "common good" principle, have now created a situation in which one fifth of the US population qualifies for government help in the shape of food stamps. One of the senior US executives I met recently in Chicago said: "I flew the other day on our corporate jet from China to Gary, Indiana, and was wondering which one is an emerging market."

Going forward, the US will have to think hard how to improve its primary and secondary education (just copy Finland please!); how to reduce the dominance and power of the financial sector (which sucks away too many smart people from more productive industries); how to reduce social inequality (which in places resembles Latin America); how to invest as a country more in

R&D than it invests now; how to prevent US multinationals from consolidating their earnings in low tax or no tax off-shore jurisdictions; and how to improve exports (the latter is about balancing the chronic current account deficit).

The big pluses for the US economy include the many great universities, world-class companies with strong innovation, entrepreneurial spirit and a "can do" attitude, and cash-rich multinationals. Many regions of the world would do well if they could imitate some of these pluses. But the minuses are worrying.

JAPAN

Even before the tragic earthquake and the nuclear disaster of 2011, the Japanese economy had struggled to find growth for years. Corporate results in terms of domestic sales reflected this. Japan was not treated like a growth market by most companies. Japan has struggled because of its "lost decade" in the 1990s and the aftermath of this. It has struggled with deflation and weak domestic spending.

Only Zimbabwe and St. Kitts and Nevis have a higher public debt as a percentage of GDP than Japan. Although the public debt is mainly domestic, its sheer size – almost 240% of GDP – means that the authorities will eventually have to start reducing it to more sustainable levels. And this will have to come through higher taxation as well as some cuts in spending. Some announcements in this direction have already been made. This will hurt growth and business in the next few years.

When the global crisis came, Japan was affected more than other regions. Its GDP fell by 6.3% in 2009. The bounce back from a low base was strong and driven by an increase of exports to strong Asian markets. GDP grew by over 4% in 2010 but then fell into recession again of 0.7% in 2011, largely as a consequence of the earthquake. Over the medium term, growth will be minimal at around 1% or in good global years slightly stronger.

3. THE RISE OF EMERGING MARKETS AND THE *RELATIVE* STAGNATION OF THE DEVELOPED WORLD

We have just arrived at a symbolic moment. After more than 150 years, emerging markets are again as large as the developed world, on the level of purchasing power parity. We have been living through a historic anomaly (due to the Industrial Revolution) in which today's developed world was bigger than today's emerging markets. This was never the case before 1850 and it will never be the case again.

Emerging markets already buy half of the world's exports and half of the world's oil. They have accumulated more than 75% of global foreign exchange reserves. This is a major buffer for future stability for many regions and countries. They are home to more than 80% of the world's population, increasing by six million people every month (as compared to 300,000 per month in the developed world, mostly in the United States through immigration).

Emerging markets are growing much faster than the developed world. For the last 15 years, on average, emerging markets outperformed the developed world in terms of growth by a margin

> **After talking to many executives during the last couple of years, the corporate consensus is clear: it will be hard to find growth in the developed world; if there is a geography that presents growth opportunity, it is definitely a broad emerging markets space.**

of about 3:1 (some countries, of course, did much better than that). This margin is likely to remain for the next decade. This crisis has actually clearly exposed something that close observers already knew was happening. Economic fundamentals show that emerging markets are in a good position compared to the developed world. Emerging Asia, the Middle East, key markets in Latin America and key markets in Central and Eastern Europe (CEE), all have better fundamentals in terms of reserves, public debt, external debt, current account balance, and budget balance than markets in Western Europe, the US or Japan. In addition, the impact of this crisis is actually accelerating the shift of economic power to emerging markets because the developed world (particularly the US and Western Europe) will have to suffer a longer post-crisis hangover period.

All of this means that sales growth in the medium term for the average multinational company will largely come from emerging markets, rather than the developed world. After talking to many executives during the last couple of years, the corporate consensus is clear: it will be hard to find growth in the developed world; if there is a geography that presents growth opportunity, it is definitely a broad emerging markets space. I will explain which emerging regions and markets will be winners in the coming years in Chapter 8.

CHAPTER 2

STRATEGIC AND STRUCTURAL SUCCESS FACTORS

In Greek myth, Icarus flew too high and his wings melted. What is the moral? Don't fly too close to the sun? Or is it, build better wings?

—*Stanley Kubrick*

"If I want sustainable profits, I am going to invest in the longer term, even if it has a negative impact on the short-term. For some of the members of the financial community, whose timeframe is between half a year or a year, it is very difficult to explain what it means to build up a business in China or Russia, where you have to invest for five to ten years before getting into profitability."

— *Peter Brabeck-Letmathe, Chairman of the Board and ex-CEO, Nestle*

THIS SECTION OF THE BOOK discusses how to build sustainable and profitable growth in emerging markets amidst the new global complexity of fast-changing competition and economic vulnerabilities. It examines the foundations for successful strategies for the future and the many things that must sit on those foundations. Compared to several years ago, the time has come for companies to engage in a significant, almost tectonic shift in strategic thinking, mindset, corporate structures and approach to emerging markets.

In my opinion, there are two key strategic foundations for future corporate success in emerging markets, and they should be present in almost everything firms do.
- The first one is how to *outperform* competition.
- And second, how to build *sustainable* sales and profit growth.

Without these foundations, corporate strategies and activities will either crumble (just like a house would collapse if built on shaky foundations), or at best, some corporate approaches will work for a while, giving executives and companies a false sense of progress and satisfaction.

And it is exactly in this "false sense of progress" sphere that many firms currently function. Most regional directors see this, but are having a hard time convincing global headquarters about the rapid changes in competitiveness that are already undermining their business in emerging markets. They also keep warning headquarters that some threats originating in emerging markets will soon come to the developed world, but very few companies are proactively thinking or guarding against this trend. Even companies with widespread geographic coverage around the world are beginning to feel vulnerable as competition, often coming from unexpected corners of the world, begins to steal away their hard-earned market shares.

THE UNPRECEDENTED RISE OF COMPETITION

Here are two quick relevant anecdotes from two of my big clients (who will for obvious reasons remain nameless).[1]

---

[1] (In agreement with the contributors, all quotes in this book are not attributed to individuals or companies.)

Every year I spend almost a full day with the global leadership of one of the largest European industrial firms, talking to them about current and future economic and business trends. And before I begin my usual session, the CEO speaks for about an hour on how the company is doing, what the major challenges are and about strategies for the future. In a meeting at the end of 2009, the CEO barely touched on competitors. Two years later in late 2011, all he did was speak about the "stunning increase in competition in all countries around the world".

He spoke about one of their Chinese competitors, who sell products under a name that is astonishingly similar to their own, and whose marketing and sales collateral is almost a copy of theirs. Most worryingly he said:

> "This is not a garbage quality product anymore. In an incredibly short space of time, the quality of their product has reached our levels. The key question for us is how should we respond when they go to our clients and offer the same product at a 40–50% discount. What worries me most is they are not only selling this product only in China, but we have seen them in Latin America, the Middle East, Africa, and most recently also in Eastern Europe."

The CEO then spoke about a group of medium-sized European firms who never ventured outside Germany or France and now they are suddenly signing up distributors in Brazil, Saudi Arabia, Indonesia and other markets – and stealing a share. And last, but not least, he spoke about Brazilian and Turkish small start-up firms with a good product and a rising influence over price-sensitive domestic customers in Brazil and Turkey.

Another anecdote comes from a US industrial company and was shared with me by a very senior executive from this firm. He was walking around the trade fair in Shanghai: "A very beautiful young Chinese lady approached me and started to chat. As a middle-aged man who likes beautiful women, I happily accepted the approach." As minutes went by he became suspicious as her questions about his firm became more focused. He bluntly asked her who she was and she calmly gave him her business card. She was working for their biggest Chinese competitor and said to him, "My job is to know everything about your company – and you."

After this he lost interest in her. He told me that this competitor was no joke. Four years ago they noticed them taking away some of their business in Asia and Africa. So the US company diligently bought the Chinese product, disassembled it and concluded that the quality was really bad and that they should not be too worried, but keep them on a radar just in case. He then added:

> "But we bought their latest product a few weeks ago and we were absolutely taken aback about how quickly they had reached our technological and quality level. Our guys on the ground throughout the world have reported that the product was currently being offered to all our customers at almost half our price. Now the challenge is what to do about this."

These two short stories illustrate a tremendous acceleration in competitive pressures in international markets, especially those that have strong economic and sales growth. But where are all these competitive pressures coming from and why is the pace of change so unusually fast?

COMPETITIVE FORCES AT WORK

There are a number of forces shaping the competitive landscape in emerging markets. The underlying reason is that all types and sizes of companies are realizing that it will be hard to grow business in the developed world in the next few years (for reasons described in the previous chapter) and all eyes are on faster-growing emerging markets. There are several groups of companies that are trying to do more in emerging markets and pushing the competitive game to new highs.

Greater focus on emerging markets by multinationals

First, traditional multinationals from the developed world are becoming more focused and systematic regarding emerging markets. They are desperate to find growth somewhere and developed markets, for many of them, are offering little or no growth. At this time and depending on the sector, 70–80% of all sales growth around the world for a typical company comes from emerging markets, and in some companies *all* growth currently comes from emerging markets. There is also a very strong corporate consensus about the future: in the next five to ten years (and probably beyond), most corporate sales growth will come from emerging markets. So many companies have concluded that they must do more in countries that are, and will continue to be, growth markets. This part of the competitive landscape, which is driven by multinationals' desperation and desire for faster growth, will get even more intense in the next decade.

All multinationals that I work with are currently thinking about and implementing strategies that will give them more growth in emerging markets. Many are moving from a relatively opportunistic to a much more systematic approach (which will be described in detail later in the book), which puts more focus, attention and investment on emerging countries. This systematization of the multinationals' efforts will build up enormous competitive pressures. Strategies and tactics that are described later in this book also show how to thrive in this new competitive intensity.

Rise of emerging market multinationals

Second, there are a growing number of emerging market companies that have regional and global ambitions. My biggest warning to all clients is to never, ever ignore *any* competitors, especially not those originating from emerging markets. Business history is full of skeletons of companies that thought the Japanese were a joke in the 1960s, or those who thought that the South Korean firms and brands were garbage some 20 years ago. Today, we observe an incredible expansion of Chinese, Indian, Brazilian, Turkish and many other firms who have outgrown their domestic markets and are also in search of growth outside of their home markets. Many of them are under pressure from multinationals at home and seek to diversify their growth through more international expansion. There are hundreds of Chinese firms and brands that will become recognized global players in the next 20 years.

Emerging market multinationals already represent 10% of Fortune 500 firms, and the percentage is rising. These emerging market multinationals are developing competitively-priced products of increasingly acceptable, even excellent, quality. Their margin objectives are different from those of large multinationals. They operate fast, with a sense of urgency and steal market share, especially during crises, when customers trade downwards anyway. They understand emerging markets more than corporate boards in the US or Western Europe, and make decisions quicker. They are used to operational obstacles and know how to overcome them. Their regard for compliance rules is sometimes lax. They poach senior executives from multinationals and double their pay to gain the expertise they lack.

They are moving in leaps and bounds. Many of my clients who run large multinationals often say how impressed they are with the ability of emerging market multinationals to expand, grow and develop rapidly. One of them, who runs an EMEA region for a major US firm, summarized this well:

> "While I sit in yet another committee in our headquarters deciding on our strategy for the Gulf, we are losing share to the Chinese, Indians and medium-sized German firms more than at any point in time. And by the time we have decided something, we will have become a minor player. And in a few years' time, my headquarters will ask me why the hell we lost market share or why are we unable to grow faster."

Perhaps the biggest differentiator from five or ten years ago is that these emerging market multinationals have good access to financing. In emerging Asia, Latin America or Turkey, local banks are in much better shape than they are in the developed world and debt financing is relatively easy to come by for local blue chip firms. Also, because most emerging markets now sit on better economic fundamentals than the developed world (see strategic regional overviews in Chapter 8), local blue chips are also finding it much easier to raise corporate bonds or get equity financing through IPOs (initial public offerings).

Some players are also clearly supported in their expansion efforts by government subsidies (usually from sovereign wealth funds or even official reserves). I do not expect this financing to dry up in the future. If anything, it will probably get even easier for locals to raise financing for international expansion. Although many of these firms are broadly good, multinationals still have an advantage over most of them, which they should capitalize on (but more on that later).

Medium sized firms focus on global expansion

Third, medium-sized (and even small) companies from the developed world have also sharply accelerated their international expansion efforts. And they are in many ways formidable and focused competitors. Medium-sized companies, like the larger ones, are also keen on growth. But they face at least three issues. Firstly, they feel they have conquered their domestic markets and need new geographic sources of growth, but are not sure how to go about it. Secondly, if they have an export business they often think it is highly volatile and not sustainable. And third, they would like to do more but are not sure how to finance a more thorough expansion. Later in the book I write about what medium-sized players should do to improve their export businesses.

But regardless of these challenges, many of my large multinational clients report how medium-sized firms from Europe, the US and other developed markets increasingly do business, even in some small and remote emerging market countries. After speaking recently at a few events in Germany, the Netherlands, Sweden, Spain, and the US organized for medium-sized firms, I can report how the number of companies interested in emerging markets is swelling fast. I am convinced that many of them will continue to look for ways to grow internationally, challenging both large multinationals and domestic players with innovative and niche products, smart positioning, smart marketing, aggressive pricing, high quality, rapid expansion and flexibility. They are adding more complexity to an already complex competitive environment.

Domestic competition

Fourth, the pure domestic players – often relatively small firms – are becoming formidable competitors and they are also increasing their operations in markets they consider their turf. One of the largest IT firms in the world said to me a few months ago that their biggest competitor in Poland (for one of their business units) is a domestic Polish firm.

I hear such stories all the time and what is often surprising is finding out how small some of these players are. But these companies are run by smart, driven entrepreneurs who benefit from good connections (and they invest a huge amount of time in building them); they are innovative, client-oriented and aggressive with pricing in order to win business and establish long-term relationships. Like emerging market multinationals, they also have more access to financing than ever before and are able to hire good people and invest in new products and services. And many are ambitious and want to one day expand beyond their domestic borders.

So the next decade will be marked by growing competitive pressures in global markets. And because of slower growth in the developed world, the largest concentration of this new, unusually lively competitive activity will be in various emerging geographies. This means that multinational firms will continue to face sales, margin and market share pressures on an unprecedented level and for many years to come. A number of well designed, well co-ordinated and well implemented strategies and actions will be needed to succeed in this new landscape. The rest of the book is largely about those strategies.

MAKING SURE YOUR EMERGING MARKETS BUSINESS IS SUSTAINABLE

Is our business sustainable in each emerging market around the world? Is our set up such that it can last and that it will help us outperform competitors for many years to come? Have we covered all bases in our strategy? How big are the barriers to entry for our competitors in emerging markets? How vulnerable is our business in these countries? These are some of the frequently asked questions

I hear during conversations with clients and during the research done for this book. Interestingly enough, most executives feel that the changes in the external environment and fast-rising competitive pressures are revealing new vulnerabilities and cracks in their strategies and structures. In other words, what for many firms initially looked like a sustainable emerging market business does not appear to be one anymore.

Only companies that build sustainable emerging markets businesses will prosper in the new, complicated global economy in the next decade and beyond. And only companies that are successful in emerging markets will deliver continuous, steady growth that will guarantee overall corporate survival over the medium and long term.

Only companies that build sustainable emerging markets businesses will prosper in the new, complicated global economy in the next decade and beyond. And only companies that are successful in emerging markets will deliver continuous, steady growth that will guarantee overall corporate survival over the medium and long term.

STRATEGIC AND STRUCTURAL ISSUES

In many companies, the next few years will be about addressing growth sustainability. Many points that will follow in this chapter describe what companies should do to build a sustainable business model in emerging markets in order to outperform the competition and deliver growth. Here are the primary strategic and structural issues.

RELENTLESS CORPORATE FOCUS ON GROWTH (OTHERWISE THE COMPETITION WILL EAT YOUR LUNCH)

Corporate leadership must ensure that exceptionally aggressive growth orientation is part of the new corporate DNA. At the same time, this should not be understood as just giving yet another series of stretch budgets to regional and country directors who run various emerging market businesses. Aggressive budgets can only deliver consistently if the foundations for future growth (as described in this chapter) are systematically put in place. I see too many exceptionally capable executives who run complicated geographies delivering one year on a stretch budget and then missing the budget the year after. And then, when we examine why, it is glaringly obvious that the business is built on shaky foundations and therefore not sustainable.

Global leadership of publicly listed firms and their frighteningly short-termist institutional owners are focused on delivering consistent quarterly and annual results. As competition rockets even more over the next few years, that consistency of earnings will be impossible to achieve without investing in solid foundations for growth in emerging markets. In many firms there is a discrepancy between how fast they want to grow in emerging markets and what has actually been invested upfront to enable that growth to occur. The goal is to continuously close that gap.

Embedding aggressive growth DNA into firms is a good thing for many reasons. Faster-growing firms increase their chance of survival. They are able to earn more, channel the money into ensuring that barriers to entry are high, and build sustainability. Employees are motivated when working on a ship that knows where it is heading and that wins the race. It is easier to keep the best and the brightest.

TREAT EMERGING MARKETS WITH AS MUCH FOCUS AS DEVELOPED WORLD MARKETS

In the past, a typical corporation spent a significantly larger proportion of their internal time and focus on developed markets than on emerging markets. This approach was understandable. Developed markets account for a larger volume of business and still had some, although slowing, growth. A global executive team simply had to make sure that the large-volume business was going well, and relatively little time was allocated to emerging markets business. Emerging markets were traditionally treated as a place that only supplemented developed world business and added to the bottom line. Emerging markets were rarely seen as crucially strategic.

> **Emerging markets were traditionally treated as a place that only supplemented developed world business and added to the bottom line.**

But staying this course today is simply too dangerous if a company wants to be a successful global player in the next decade. Responsible CEOs cannot just think about the next few quarters. Business in the developed world, although still representing the largest sales volume for a typical multinational company, is barely growing for most firms. And relative to emerging markets it will slow down further in the next few years (see Chapter 1).

The time has come for companies to move to the next level of systematizing their business in emerging markets with a sustained approach. While this systematization effort has many aspects (which I will address throughout this book), one underlying factor is incredibly important. At the global level, emerging markets must receive the same seriousness, focus, and attention as the developed world. These days, this often means that emerging markets are getting a larger-than-usual proportion of corporate business development funds.

BUILD AND NURTURE A "TWO HEADED MONSTER"

There are two obvious corporate temptations these days, and both are wrong. First, in some companies there is the temptation and determination to focus massive resources on emerging markets, clearly at the expense of developed markets. Second, in some companies there is the temptation and determination to protect one's existing business (largely in the developed world), at the expense of any systematic expansion in emerging markets (or worse, treat emerging markets as a place where you just squeeze them for short-term profits).

The problem with these approaches is that they risk future business in both the developed world and emerging markets. A corporation of the future should be a little bit like that funny film starring Steve Martin, *The Man with Two Brains*. A company of the future must become a "two headed monster": one head focusing on protecting (and growing if possible) the large-volume, low-growth markets of the developed world; the other on building medium- and long-term market positions in emerging markets. This is really about having two different mindsets. And both heads need to talk to each other and exchange experiences more than ever. Down the road, as emerging markets become richer, the two heads will merge, but this is many decades away. Without strategic focus and commitment, no company has ever outperformed the competition in emerging markets on a sustainable basis. The emerging markets "brain" should be much more long-term in its outlook.

One way that companies are developing the "two-headed monster" is to appoint a head of emerging markets, so that the newly-found focus and attention is not lost as time goes by. The head of emerging markets reports directly to the CEO and under him has regional heads for emerging Asia, Latin America, Sub-Saharan Africa, Middle East North Africa (MENA) and Central Eastern Europe (CEE). Within those regions, many firms have also developed regional sub-clusters (groups of countries that share similarities and a number of fixed costs for non-face-to-face business functions).

Companies who have made this internal structural shift find that emerging market regions get a fair and proper hearing at the global level, and most importantly, markets get resource allocations based on their own merit. For example, if a regional executive running a Middle East set-up argues for more resources for the fast-growing Saudi Arabian market, a company that is not structured as a "two headed monster" might send a message to the regional head: "We are in cost-cutting mode in the developed world, so no new resources for Saudi." First of all, this should not happen in a company that wants to grow its global business. Second, it is less likely to happen in a company that is structured in a way that systematically nurtures emerging market business opportunities.

AVOID MIXING DEVELOPED WORLD AND EMERGING MARKETS CORPORATE STRUCTURES

Many firms have learned the hard way that having one person running North America and Latin America, or one person running Western Europe and Central Eastern Europe, is not good for corporate sales growth in emerging markets. The big developed markets are so significant in terms of size that anyone running Western Europe spends most of his or her time doing that and not having enough time to focus on an array of smaller markets in Central Eastern Europe. As a result, such companies often under-penetrate emerging markets and underperform the competition. They also grow less and hold sometimes ridiculously low market shares compared to the global strength of their brands.

In an ideal world of strong focus on building sustainable business in emerging markets, companies should have the regional heads who run emerging market regions report directly to the CEO or head of emerging markets rather than having single heads straddling EMEA (Europe, Middle East and Africa), the Americas or the Asia Pacific.

In a less ideal, but acceptable structure for the future, companies can retain their, for example, head of EMEA, provided that under him there is another layer of regional managers, each in charge of Sub-Saharan Africa, the Middle East and North Africa, Central Eastern Europe and Western Europe. Equally, having a head of the Americas is acceptable, provided there is someone appointed regional head for Latin America who lives and dies in that territory. Within the Asia Pacific, at the minimum there should separate heads for Japan and the rest of emerging Asia (although more and more companies rightfully treat China, and increasingly India, as separate entities that report directly to global HQ).

I call this a less ideal structure because many of my clients have noticed how their message from CEE or MENA markets sent to the top gets modified through the overall EMEA structure, where Western Europe concerns are so overwhelming. This is why I say to companies that the ideal structure is for emerging market regional heads to report directly to global HQ, so that a true picture of the market goes straight to the top, raw and undiluted. If the message is getting through, it will be easier to make decisions about which markets deserve more resources, why product portfolios need changing, or why we have to pay our top staff in Russia more than in Austria.

AVOID CORPORATE SHORT-TERMISM

If you look at the Fortune 500 list from some 25 years ago compared to today, you will notice that only some 40% of the companies are still on the list. An astonishing 60% of firms are no longer there. And yet so many companies assume they will automatically survive over the next couple of decades. Considering the massive rise in competitive pressures from all corners, the rate of corporate failures is going to increase at an ever-growing pace. And smart corporate strategies must guard against this. Owning a sustainable business in emerging markets should be an essential part of the corporate strategy, but to make sure this happens, global leadership teams have to establish a different communication channel to its investors (life in this respect is easier for privately-owned firms and largely debt-financed European and Japanese firms, as they can usually take a more long-term perspective).

The key communication point to stock investors (many of whom these days do not behave like investors but more like herd-driven speculators) is to patiently explain the plan to build market leadership in global markets, that this will cost money, and that it will lower earnings per share over the next 12–18 quarters. The key message is that investment in building stronger international business will ensure stronger and more consistent earnings streams over the medium and long term.

I have seen many boards getting very nervous about this idea, wondering how Wall Street is going to react and fearing a collapse of their share price. But any corporate leadership, if it wants to ensure long-term prosperity, must avoid falling into the quarterly earnings game. Pursuing quarterly earnings has weakened a number of companies over the years and it has literally destroyed international business ambitions in many of them. I work with companies that are among the top three players in their home markets in Europe and the US, but they are number 11 in Turkey, or number 14 in Chile. You know such firms consistently under-invest in their emerging markets business. When I was asked by one US CEO back in early 2011 what to do about their short-term investors, I joked and told him: "Tell Wall Street to go to hell – but politely."

Sadly, we have also seen over the years how some corporate leaders continue to maximize short-term quarterly returns to please their investors and to ensure they benefit personally from lucrative stock option plans. The shelf life of a typical CEO is getting shorter every year: consequently, many, when they finally reach the top, want to make sure they reap the biggest personal benefits. Corporate boards should recognize such individuals early enough and respond accordingly.

ENGAGE IN LONG-RANGE PLANNING FOR EMERGING MARKETS

There are more companies engaging in ten year planning for growth in emerging markets than ever before. Many senior executives now feel the need to create a road map for an extended period of time that will guide strategic and operational planning. One of senior executive said to me recently:

> "When we have a three year plan, we somehow always achieve what we set to achieve. But today, three years is not enough. Three years still drives our guys to think too much about quarters, and then we find ourselves postponing certain growth initiatives during any external setbacks. Ten years is a good horizon and we have a plan called Vision 2020. While this sounds like boring, corporate vision 'blah blah', it is actually useful because I know it will force all of us to think how to get there. The most important aspect of the plan is that it maps the manufacturing, marketing, HR and other investments that we need to make. And without those upfront, smart investments, we can only dream about dominating those markets."

SHIFT TO LONG-TERM CORPORATE INVESTMENTS IN EMERGING MARKETS

Another executive from one of the largest consumer goods firms in the world says their long-range planning has just experienced another twist.

> "We are one of the few firms that has been doing long-range planning for emerging markets and I can tell it has served us incredibly well. Now we have long-range plans for almost every country in the emerging world. I can tell you today what we are planning to do in Kenya in 2016 or Mexico in 2018. It is that detailed and it includes new manufacturing plants, product launches, numbers of staff – you name it. Of course, only some major political disruptions can change this but for that we also have contingency plans in place. It is a road map that keeps people motivated."

In other interviews with companies, another theme emerged as a benefit of long-range plans. The hope is that plans will make the business resistant to rising competition, especially if the plans call for a deeper local presence of face-to-face business functions (and good plans do). Also, long-range planning is an effective retention tool. It is much easier to build teamwork and to motivate employees when there is a unified purpose – a clear goal ahead. It gets the competitive juices flowing and it helps regional and local execution, as long as short-term growth targets are reasonable and realistic.

Within those long-range plans companies should ask themselves if they have a plan for Indonesia, Turkey or Russia for the next 10 years. Or if they have a plan for Africa (most companies do not and wonder how to go about it, by the way). Long-range planning has to be at the regional and country level – and as detailed and well researched as possible. The key is also to understand underlying economic drivers in order to make reasonably accurate assumptions about the future.

ENABLE THE EXECUTION OF LONG-RANGE PLANS

It is dangerous to simply talk about grand visions for emerging markets, but then not follow up on what is needed in terms of upfront investment. And sadly, too many firms are still masters at doing precisely that. They pay lip service that in the end hurts not only poor regional and country executives, who struggle to achieve consistent sales growth, but companies suffer over all, too.

Many firms that I have worked with over the last couple of years have actually put some of their long-range plans on hold, and many initiatives are waiting to be implemented. Of course, some of the delays had to do with the impact of the global financial and economic crisis, and if this is so, then delays are justifiable. However, many are just part of the good old corporate tradition of coming up with grand plans for emerging markets but not following up with actual investments. One regional executive summarized this well:

"The company has not really followed up in terms of investments that were scheduled in those nice-looking PowerPoint slides that we presented to the CEO and he approved. But I am still expected to deliver the growth targets. This is the easiest way to encourage loyal and committed executives to think about leaving. It is hugely de-motivating."

BOARD DIVERSIFICATION IS ESSENTIAL TO BROADEN CORPORATE HORIZONS

"Ever since we brought a Brazilian to sit on our global board, our understanding and investments into Latin America have gone up and up, and the returns have been phenomenal." I have heard comments like this quite often over recent years. More and more firms realize that nationally uniform boards simply keep the horizons too narrow. Naturally there are prejudices against all or some emerging markets. People remember economic crises during the 1990s in Mexico, Asia, Brazil and Russia, and think these places are too risky and not worth the sustained effort. Prejudices remain but many are wrong and/or based on some negative past experience (usually badly executed).

In one board meeting where I spoke recently, one of the board members explained how the company had once tried Central Eastern Europe, did not do well and pulled out. He was against re-entering this market. When I probed about how the entry was carried out and what had happened, it was clear that the previous approach was largely wrong, with very little upfront investment and relying on "fly-in, fly-out", management from a distance. They underinvested and were eaten alive by more systematic competitors.

New board members who originate from emerging economies or have had long experience in those geographies can add tremendous value to corporate strategies and most importantly, counter various unhelpful prejudices. The quality of board debates increases and emerging economies get a larger share of attention. Diversified board debates will appreciate emerging market opportunities and realize that in fact most risks in emerging markets are manageable with the right approach, structure and corporate guidelines. The new board members from emerging markets, or those who understand them well, can also identify serious risks that may not be visible from a distance, and prevent the company from doing something stupid – something that goes against best practice or is simply way too risky.

MAKE SURE THAT THE EXECUTIVE CORPORATE LEADERSHIP FULLY SUPPORTS STRONGER UPFRONT INVESTMENTS IN EMERGING MARKETS

In addition to having boards supporting the build-up of sustainable business structures in emerging markets, it is essential to have a fully committed executive team, and not just the CEO. Regional directors report that their expansion plans were fully implemented only when the whole leadership team was behind expansion, enabling full deployment of the necessary resources. Several companies I have met over the years have said that just CEO commitment is not enough. Often, the number two or three in the firm are not fully behind the move, and then seek to undermine the expansion plans because they are worried about the cost having a short-term impact on their share price. Without the full, global executive leadership team providing *real* support, many firms fail to build a sustainable business in emerging markets. Such firms will be in for a nasty surprise in the next few years as other competitors from all corners of the world become more systematic and aggressive.

So when regional directors try to create a coherent voice that will be clearly heard at the top, they must ensure that key corporate officers visit the markets in question, see the business and local staff in action and appreciate the opportunities – but also understand the size of investment needed to make it work.

DO NOT EXPECT AUTOMATIC MARKET LEADERSHIP – INSTEAD, NURTURE AN UPFRONT INVESTMENT CULTURE AND PROACTIVE, SUSTAINED BRAND-BUILDING

One of the most frequent complaints I hear from regional directors is that many headquarters are enthusiastic about emerging markets but often do not follow up in terms of necessary upfront investment to make things happen. I have written before about corporate arrogance and this is a feature of emerging market business that is still, sadly, alive and well. Many firms assume that if their brands are known in the developed world that somehow they will be equally and instantly recognized and bought in emerging markets. They assume that market leadership will be practically automatic.

But while this might be true for a few truly global brands, it is far from the truth for most others. Ironically, it is those best-known brands that are often the least arrogant and invest enormous amounts of money in building and nurturing all aspects of their brands. In my experience, the Nestlés and Cokes of this world are masters of sustainable brand-building and have the least complacent attitude.

Others, who assume automatic leadership and do not nurture upfront investment, proceed at their own peril. Perhaps this arrogant expectation of automatic market leadership would have worked in the past, when local market competition was weak, but those days are clearly gone as competitive pressures increase, day in, day out.

DEEPEN COUNTRY-LEVEL PRESENCE, INFRASTRUCTURE, CAPABILITIES AND COMPETENCIES – REGIONAL STRATEGIES ARE NOT ENOUGH

To build lasting success in international business in the future, companies must invest in exceptionally deep local infrastructure, competencies and capabilities. Many executives that I am in frequent contact with think they should be better resourced in quite a few markets around the world. There is a strong sense that unless this is done, it will be hard to nurture key relationships, to understand consumers and customers and how they evolve, to build constant bridges with governments, and to engage in sharp local execution and marketing/sales excellence.

It is very clear that companies need sophisticated country-level strategies and that a purely regional approach is simply not enough anymore. Too many companies are very precise about their regional strategy and not precise enough about their deeper, country-level strategy. They often leave their country-level strategy to local general managers – or much worse, just distributors – without fully understanding the full resourcing needs or appreciating growth potential. Regional strategy as an overarching guide, yes; but unless companies engage much deeper into local markets in the future, they leave an incredible amount of space for the competition to move in. That is simply too risky, considering an incredible rise in competitive pressures.

While this point sounds in parts like the old cliché, "think global, act local", it is really more about making sure you have enough local infrastructure and the right people with the requisite competencies and capabilities in place; without this, any local execution will be inadequate at best. In the words of one of my bigger clients in the food and beverage sector:

> "In the next decade there will be three important things for us in emerging markets: local execution, local execution and local execution. Thank God I am retiring next year. It will be hard work!"

MAKE SURE THAT THE CORPORATE LEADERSHIP IS AWARE OF THE SHEER NUMBER OF EMERGING MARKET OPPORTUNITIES – AND CHALLENGES

While many senior executives talk about emerging markets with growing enthusiasm, in many firms grand words are not followed with proper resourcing. Experienced regional directors know that the best way to win resources is to make sure that the senior leadership visits as many markets around the world as possible, talking to customers, consumers and other firms and personally feel the pulse of the market. Such visits often end up increasing enthusiasm and with it the allocation of resources. And what is important, it helps the senior leadership appreciate the market's potential, which is important when it comes to resource allocation during global crunches.

When sales struggle in the developed world, it is easy for the senior leadership who do not have an appreciation for emerging markets to say: "You need resources for Turkey? You must be joking. Don't you know we are in a cost-cutting mode in Italy and the United States?" But companies with a senior leadership that understand and appreciate emerging markets do not fall into this short-termist trap. After all, it is critical to invest resources into markets based on their own merit and growth potential, rather than what is happening elsewhere. As I explain in chapter 8, many emerging markets will do well in the future and easily outperform economic growth rates in developed markets.

It is critical to invest resources into markets based on their own merit and growth potential, rather than what is happening elsewhere.

While it is usually incredibly beneficial for companies when regional directors take global leaders to visit their regions, it is important for regional leaders not to oversell certain regions and countries. In other words, also show the CEO and his global team the downsides of the markets – the poor and risky areas. If the message is not balanced, regional directors usually end up with enormous stretch budgets that make their targets hard to achieve.

DECENTRALIZE DECISION MAKING, BUT NOT TO THE EXTREME

International business history indicates companies often go international by moving from one extreme to the other. They start with a heavily centralized structure – heavy in global and regional centres in terms of resources and resource-light at a local level. In such situations, almost every decision is referred to the centre. After a while, companies realize that this is not going to work, so they create country-level kingdoms with self-contained infrastructures and almost total decision-making authority.

Both approaches are wrong. In the first, nothing is sustainable and it is just a good start that will not last very long. In the second, deep local infrastructure can be very good for sales and marketing as well as an overall understanding of the markets; but at the same time, there have been firms in the past where country managers did not even have to go back to their headquarters when they wanted to build factories. They just built them, which lead to massive inefficiencies in manufacturing and R&D. It also led to inefficient fixed-cost structures.

The best structure in terms of decision making that I recommend to my clients (simply because it is showing the best results for the top and bottom line), is to give more responsibility, accountability and decision-making power to country managers, but at the same time make sure that there are clear guidelines they cannot cross (such as decisions on manufacturing, or decisions on what the brand or the products stands for). Some of the fastest-growing companies in emerging markets are those that allow their country managers to hire as they see fit. They are given significant freedom. Marketing and sales are very localized in such structures in terms of execution.

Allowing extra responsibility and accountability does wonders when it comes to motivating country-level leaders. When the global crisis spilled over into Central Eastern Europe, some regional directors said to their country heads: "This is your country. You know it best. You figure out how to avoid a collapse in sales. You figure out how to grow. It is your baby." Those regional directors report that motivation levels jumped to new highs. As one global leader told me in the US recently:

> "My country manager in Brazil has always been telling me that all he wants from me is to leave him alone to deliver. I finally caved in during the crisis and he has flourished. The results have just gone through the roof ever since headquarters got out of his sight."

INCREASE ON-THE-GROUND RESOURCES FOR FACE-TO-FACE BUSINESS FUNCTIONS AND MANAGE BACK OFFICE FUNCTIONS IN CENTRALIZED OR REGIONAL CLUSTERS

Giving more responsibility and decision-making power to country managers does not necessarily have to be accompanied by a higher fixed-cost base. There is no reason to have all business functions in each market. That would be a waste of resources.

It is essential that face-to-face functions are well represented in local markets. Many marketing elements, sales and government relations should cover all the local bases and be focused on local execution. In other words, our brands stand for something, but on the ground we figure the best way to market and sell them.

At the same time, all back office functions that do not require face-to-face contact can be put in regional or sub-regional support offices. These could be in-house shared service centres or even outsourced shared service centres (although many companies have reservations about outsourcing certain functions, such as receivables chasing with long-standing customers).

FLEXIBILITY IN APPROACH AND STRUCTURES

Business is moving too fast in emerging markets. Many regional directors of multinationals think their approach is too rigid and not responsive to the actual market needs and realities. Forget about, "We do not do it this way." and make sure that each market is approached in such a way as to maximize sales, market share and profit growth in a sustainable way. If this means doing things that a company does not normally do, but would be a good idea locally, then why not go for it? (This obviously does not apply to compliance issues!)

If the approach works, spread the word quickly to all markets. Regional directors of major multinationals often see their own firms as similar to massive tankers that take forever to turn, accelerate or stop. And while the tanker is trying to move in the right direction, more agile competitors are grabbing the market with incredible speed.

"While our corporate planning meetings failed to agree on anything, we lost not only market share in many countries, but also passed up on several strategic acquisitions that would have made us a real player in Asia and Latin America", says one regional director of a US multinational company.

A particular threat to multinationals' slowness and rigidity comes not only from emerging market multinationals, but also purely domestic competitors.

"They are giving us a serious run for our money. This is no longer a story of a small, annoying group of competitors. Their quality has improved immensely, their speed of decision-making is phenomenal and they have poached dozens of executives from our company in the last two years. They pay really well and we must do something about it urgently," says a regional director of a European firm based in Geneva.

While a regional director of a multinational company in Dubai advises:

"To improve our business in the Gulf and CIS markets, we concluded we needed strong teams of government relations professionals in almost every market. Here, nothing gets done in the public sector without strong links to government officials. But the headquarters rejected the idea because our global rules say some of these markets are too small to justify government relations professionals."

This is a typical example of a company putting useless global rules ahead of what business really needs on the ground to grow in the future. Such companies are shooting themselves in the foot and leaving the door wide open for competition.

GEOGRAPHIC LEADERSHIP AND ACCOUNTABILITY IS A CRUCIAL PIECE OF THE GROWTH PUZZLE

These are the words of the CEO of one of the largest multinationals during a recent meeting:

> "We have six large global business units and when I took over this multinational, I was surprised that one unit was superbly established in emerging markets, two were reasonably well established, one was doing something via distributors and two were only active in the EU and US. When I spoke with global heads of those business units I realized that some were interested in international business and others were just managing what they had quarter to quarter, unwilling to take any growth risks. I did two things quickly. First, I told all heads of global units that they must go global in a way one of our successful units has done. Second, to assist that global expansion, I quickly installed heads of geography in five emerging regions, tasked them with finding growth and gave them P&L responsibility for regional growth of all our businesses. Heads of geography and heads of business units now work closely together in terms of finding growth. We made this change three years ago and everyone has

been surprised by how much new business we found once we put the geographic focus in place and once all our business divisions were proactively chasing opportunities. Also, we are now able to spread our fixed costs over all business units, and not just two or three. The ultimate result is that we are now growing faster than ever in a more efficient way."

There is enough anecdotal evidence to demonstrate that companies with many business units underperform if they do not have a geographic focus, i.e., if just heads of global business units decide what will be done without working at a local level. The key is to have a clear mandate for geographic leaders as well as a good team spirit between geographic heads and global heads of business units.

Clear regional accountability is important and it forces heads of geographic areas to find new sources of growth. In other words they "live and die" in a territory and have a huge vested interest to succeed. At the same time, the structure has to be such as to keep nurturing all business units in a geography. In other words, the company is failing if, for example, overall regional results are better than last year but along the way, three business units are not doing well.

To boost growth prospects further, several companies I know well have now installed regional growth project leaders who report to heads of geographic areas and are tasked with proactively uncovering growth opportunities throughout their respective regions. Needless to say, this geographic accountability is also essential at a country level.

THINK CREATIVELY ABOUT FINANCING EMERGING MARKETS EXPANSION

It is not a resource-light exercise to expand properly to world markets and to build a sustainable business. Resource-light expansions tend to hurt results over time, especially measured against the competition (not in all industries, though – hotel brands can still expand without investing in resources and use just management contract expansion). Many firms wonder how to finance expansion or are reluctant to dip into cash reserves during these uncertain economic times. Although most multinationals were hit hard when the global crisis started, a few years later, most of them are sitting on record amounts of cash, but are reluctant to spend. US firms have more cash reserves than at any time in the last 50 years.

But smart companies should dip into those cash reserves now and build a corporation that will command market shares in countries around the world. The period of slow growth in the developed world (which will go on well beyond 2012) is actually a fantastic window of opportunity to invest for long-term success in international markets. While many firms are sleeping on mountains of cash, those that invest now in a focused way will be the winners of emerging market business in the future.

It is also time to look at financing international operations in a more creative way. Many firms are issuing, or thinking about issuing, new shares and corporate bonds in emerging markets. How many readers know that Nestlé is listed not only in Switzerland but also in India, Malaysia, Nigeria, Pakistan, Sri Lanka and Serbia? Local investors in emerging markets are keen on buying new IPOs or corporate bonds of known international companies. Most new corporate bond issues are denominated in domestic currencies, which is smart. It is important to match the liability currency with the currency in which the domestic revenues will be made. One of the things that hurt many firms in the past is that they had debt exposure in currencies other than domestic. And when domestic currencies depreciated, it was hard to service debts and growth initiatives had to be put on hold.

Companies actually prefer corporate bonds and debt over local IPOs. While local IPOs can bring wonderful amounts of money that can be invested in developing the emerging markets, they are also more complex, since those firms also need local boards – and some global boards feel uncomfortable about that.

In any case, the sources of financing for international expansion are still alive and well, at least for very large firms. For medium-sized firms this is not so easy and I examine these issues later in Chapter 7.

DO NOT FINANCE YOUR COUNTRY-LEVEL EXPANSION JUST WITH EARNINGS GENERATED FROM THOSE COUNTRIES

The biggest expansion mistakes of the last 20 years has been made by those firms who say to their regional and country level people: "I will give you more resources once I see you generate bigger sales…." This kind of instruction usually originates from CEOs that are obsessed with quarterly earnings for one reason or another. Such companies have traditionally trailed those that invested upfront and sustainably, and then patiently waited for returns for several years. Those firms who continue with the same short-term approach are on the way to losing market share in emerging markets in the coming years. There is too much competition today for such an approach to succeed.

It is important to use funding for expansion from global corporations (or other debt/equity sources), because initially you won't make enough money in an individual region or country to carry out proper expansion that will lead to a sustainable business and outperform the competition.

SUSTAIN GROWTH INITIATIVES

"We had a wonderful growth plan for CEEMEA that my team was enthusiastic about. It seemed realistic to me, with plenty of scheduled investments to increase and deepen our local presence and the ability to execute. Then the corporation missed the quarterly earnings but was still enormously profitable and was growing. But four out of our six initiatives were promptly postponed. However, I was still expected to deliver the same stretch budget, which of course, proved to be possible on the profit side only if I savagely cut costs, including laying off some great people. So practically overnight we went from being growth driven to cost-cutting driven. The irony was that the global CEO still spoke about the growth agenda. Those of us on the ground knew this was the ultimate nonsense that hurt not only that year

Only companies that maintain growth initiatives will be able to build sustainable business growth.

but the year after. This, for me, is a prime example of bad, short-termist corporate leadership."

This story, which was shared with me over dinner in Paris, is just one example of many similar stories I have heard in recent years. Only companies that maintain growth initiatives will be able to build sustainable business growth.

NEVER EVER IGNORE ANY COMPETITOR – REBUILD COMPETITIVE INTELLIGENCE TO A POINT OF SUPERIORITY

I explained earlier in this chapter the sources of huge current and expected growth in competitive pressures in all emerging markets. But too many companies still merely track their obvious large multinational competitors and only sporadically observe other players, usually with some surprise. One of the most impressive pieces of competitive intelligence structure I saw last year was developed by one large EU-based multinational, which created an internal team that, through their local offices and help from distributors, tracked all competitors in each market in the world. As they built a database and monitoring system, they found it completely astonishing that the number of competitors in each market was 38–74% larger (that was the range depending on the market) than they had originally anticipated.

In each market, they have an internal competitive intelligence officer who tracks everything about each competitor: any new products coming in and how they are positioned, new pricing promotions, any structural changes, key staff movements, new advertising campaigns, new competitors, etc.

"We thought we knew our competition well, but this exercise proved that we were crap. Now we finally understand who is eating away, or trying to eat away, our market positions in each product category. Before we invested in this system we were just guessing, relying on some local agencies to identify market shares, and our executive response was equally imprecise. Now we are so much smarter in terms of our new product strategies, promotional activities and positioning. The best thing about it is that it's enthusiastically accepted by our CEO, and crucially it is guiding our new product development."

(There will be more on how firms must improve marketing excellence – an important issue these days – later in the book.)

SPEED AND URGENCY MUST BE PART OF AN EMERGING MARKETS APPROACH

Many country and regional level managers complain about how slow their companies move. They observe business and competition move at lightning speed in many markets while "we seem to be asleep at the wheel", in the words of one of my long-standing clients. While there are many different moans, perhaps the crucial complaint is linked to lack of product development that would match the actual market needs of the specific country. Other complaints include a lack of understanding for the high prices paid for local staff (as a result of tight supply and huge demand), and an inability to quickly deploy resources to high-growth areas.

Companies that do not entrench speed and urgency in their corporate DNA from the very top to junior sales level, will find it enormously hard to gain share and to grow in a sustainable way in emerging markets.

FORGET FLY-IN, FLY-OUT MANAGEMENT AND INCREASE LOCAL CONTROL OVER YOUR BUSINESS

In late 2011, I was sitting in the EMEA headquarters of one of the largest information technology firms in the world. The goal of the meeting was to see how the firm could grow faster in Central and Eastern Europe. They had good growth, despite the challenging economic times, but were keen on accelerating it.

As we dug deeper into the structure and approach, I was astonished that such a large firm had local offices in only seven out of 28 markets in the region. Twenty-one markets were being run by just one person sitting in their European headquarters, and he and his small team were coordinating a daunting network of local partners and distributors from a distance. They were gaining share or maintaining a stable position in markets with local presence, but they were losing it in these 21 markets run by the poor "fly-in, fly-out" guy (who, by the way, looked more exhausted than anyone I've seen in years). The control of the business was minimal; the knowledge of local consumers and customers poor; someone else owned the relationships with key clients; marketing was distant and not connected to local needs; distributors were sometimes focused on the business and sometimes not; prices were inconsistent; and product awareness/understanding/loyalty was low, especially when it came to new product launches.

This distant approach to business in certain geographies still plagues a surprising number of large firms. This is for at least two reasons: first, regional directors are unable to convince short-termist global directors to make the investment; and second, many firms did reasonably well until recently with this approach and find it hard to believe that the game has changed that much. As I have argued earlier, the pace of competitive change is such that "fly-in, fly-out" management simply does not work well enough anymore. It has never been the right approach for sustainability. In the future, as competition intensifies even more, the "fly-in, fly-out" system will quickly lead to sharp market share losses and a complete inability to grow in such geographies. The sooner companies embrace the urgent need to be more local, in as many countries as possible, the better their future prospects will be.

CLOSE GEOGRAPHIC GAPS PROACTIVELY AND FOCUS ON SMALLER COUNTRIES

After travelling to over 90 countries around the world and talking to numerous executives over the years, I came to the conclusion that there is good business potential almost everywhere, including in some really small and poor countries. One of my clients recently landed a US $40 million deal to sell equipment in Sierra Leone, exceeding in size any deal they managed in Russia the same year (although not for the lack of trying in Russia). Another IT firm is currently making more money in Georgia than in Turkey, because there is less competition in Georgia. A European bank I know consistently makes more profit in Albania than in the Czech Republic. And it goes on and on.

The above-mentioned firms were keen on Russia, Turkey and the Czech Republic and had bigger operations and more resources invested than in Sierra Leone, Georgia or Albania. But one of the great advantages of being equally focused on smaller countries is that there is usually much less competition. Once personal relationships are well established with key customers and governments, it is quite difficult for competitors to come in. And relative lack of competition also means that many firms are able to charge higher prices in some smaller markets than in larger ones. Just ask South African retailers what their margins are in some of the small Sub-Saharan markets. And then ask German or French retailers about their margins at home.

ONE MAN AND HIS DOG

To take advantage of the smaller markets' potential (and be well positioned for their stronger growth and size in the future), companies should not only sign up distributors on the ground but also initially open small sales/marketing offices that will liaise with local government and customers, but also liaise very closely with distributors and consumers. As I have argued in this book, nothing can really be a substitute for some physical local presence. Since global boards tend to be reluctant to approve new office openings in Albania or Sierra Leone, I encourage my clients to sell this internally as a "one man and his dog" approach that really does not cost much but where the benefits are tremendous, especially over the medium and long term.

There are at least three things that usually happen once companies open such small offices, with literally one person on the ground initially.

- First, this one person discovers there is much more business on the ground than their distributor was telling them before (remember that distributors are always distracted with other things, and may have their own interests).
- Second, the business improves quite quickly as one person engages in marketing and sales initiatives and as he improves on the distributors' way of doing things.
- And third, very soon firms realize that one person on the ground is not enough and that more resources on the sales and marketing side are needed. Companies that do this genuinely build significantly more sustainable business in such markets than those firms that continue to work from a distance.

My advice to companies is to abandon their global "rule books", which often dictate at which point-of-sale size a particular market qualifies for a local office. One of my long-standing clients summarized this corporate view well:

> "Every time I tried to open new offices in a few small countries in Central America, the answer from the corporate head was that it did not qualify under corporate rules because the sales were still too low. We were stuck in a classic chicken-and-egg situation. This was one of the many global rules that no one dared to question for a long time. But I was not the only frustrated regional manager. Me and my colleagues

in charge of Africa, the Middle East, Latin America and Asia were all convinced that we must build greater sustainability in every market around the world, so we created a joint presentation for the CEO, arguing that this rule be scrapped and that we needed to take this relatively inexpensive leap. After all, we are working for a corporation that was annually spending a billion or two on acquisitions, but was reluctant to invest tens of millions on 50 to 60 small sales/marketing offices. We eventually won the argument and now are in the phase of pushing our small local presence through rep offices in 12 countries this year and 28 next year."

RELATIONSHIP-BUILDING IS CRITICAL

Any old business hand will tell you how critical relationships are in emerging markets. (This is why so much of my argument so far is about developing good relationships.) Only those firms whose managers build deep relationships with customers, governments and other stakeholders will be able to have long-term sustainable business in emerging markets. And this is not possible without a very deep local presence for all face-to-face business functions.

Many firms that I work with realize that in many markets it is their distributors who hold the key relationships. The risk is that if a distributor relationship goes sour, a company will be without key customer relationships, at least for a while. Ideally, it should be country managers and their top lieutenants who build and nurture client relationships. Remember that personal relationships often precede business relationships in many emerging markets. And it is important to have enough resources to nurture relationships, even with buyers who are currently not buying anything. Do not only call your customers when you want them to buy something....

I cannot emphasize enough how important it is for firms to treat relationship-building as an ongoing priority, and to make sure enough is invested to enable this to happen. Whether this means adding more government-relations people in certain markets or opening new offices in new geographies, it should all be part of the same goal of long-term business sustainability. Do not underestimate the cost of relationship building.

It is important to build relationship with governments and other officials even if you do not have public sector business interests. This is because markets can be so difficult operationally that you often need "friends" in the right places to be able to overcome regular operational difficulties.

USE YOUR STRENGTHS TO COMPETE AGAINST EMERGING MARKET MULTINATIONALS

While new companies from unexpected corners of the world provide increasingly tough and serious competition, it is important for multinationals not to squander their current advantages over such competition in the next few years. And big global players have many strengths, such as larger cash reserves, typically stronger brands, usually bigger marketing and sales expertise and better trained leaders and managers. But all these advantages will go to waste if firms do not deploy them in a proactive and urgent way.

Too many firms now sit on record amounts of cash, but many do just that – they sit on cash and do not deploy it in growth markets that deserve more resources. Also, still too many firms own wonderful brands but are not doing enough to turn these brands into market leaders in all geographical regions. And so many firms have superb marketing and sales expertise, but still leave so many of their geographies covered by just local partners and distributors. Global competition is becoming so intense that unless such multinationals start proactively and urgently using their advantages, they will lose them quickly as new competitors get stronger and bigger.

IF YOU ARE AN EMERGING MARKET MULTINATIONAL READING THIS, EXPLOIT THE WEAKNESSES OF BIG GLOBAL PLAYERS

Many regional and country level executives who work for major global players are deeply worried that their firms are moving too slowly, not investing enough upfront in emerging markets and not really responding to market needs. Some refer to their companies as "tankers" that are impossible to turn quickly. Others call them "short-termist nut houses", where quarterly earnings and internal politics matter more than international customers. "Our CEO treats emerging markets merely as a cash cow – extract as much profit, pay lip service to sustainability," complains a regional director of one of the big US multinationals.

Emerging market multinationals clearly have an opportunity against a few short-termist global players who are slow to recognize domestic needs in markets around the world or too slow to build a sustainable business. In some places the gaps that large global players leave are substantial. These gaps can be geographic, structural (not enough local presence or focus), product-based (too narrow a product portfolio to serve multiple market segments), or in terms of marketing, being too distant.

ACCELERATE KNOWLEDGE EXCHANGE WITHIN A FIRM

A number of companies are quickly institutionalizing knowledge exchange within their firms. As new ideas are rolled out across many markets (with the goal of accelerating sales growth and gaining share), companies are trying to make sure that an idea that worked well in, for example, Argentina or Indonesia, is quickly known around the world. When global competition was not as complicated as it is today, it was enough for regional teams to meet once or twice a year and exchange experiences about which initiatives worked and which did not. This is certainly not enough anymore. I recommend to my clients to create internal, small knowledge centres in the headquarters that are in regular contact with regional and country directors, collecting wisdom, best practices and internal initiatives, and then spread this knowledge around the world. At the various annual or biannual corporate retreats, more time should be spent on good discussion of case studies from different regions. As a regional director of a large European multinational says:

> "Life is more complicated than ever and we have to work so much harder than before to prosper. This is why it is so important to use everyone's creative juices and new ideas. Some of the best marketing ideas we recently rolled out globally came from our offices

in South Africa and Ukraine, interestingly enough. When you think about it, this is not that surprising. Those guys constantly need to invent new things just to survive. They think differently, and luckily we have a system in place that quickly recognizes ideas that no one has thought of before."

Many firms are building tried-and-tested databases of best practices, based on observing what their competitors and non competitors have been doing. And they proactively announce to teams around the world when something new and exciting is developed. Global leadership should be the big users of these best practices databases. Quite a few global leaders have told me in the last few years that, because of all the pressures, they often feel at least partly disconnected from trends in emerging markets, and this is a good way to keep in touch with market trends and best practices.

LEARN FROM OTHER FIRMS

More and more firms feel that harvesting new internal knowledge is no longer enough to stay ahead of the competitive game. In addition to the already mentioned improvement of competitive intelligence, companies should seek to join any events where they can find out what other firms are doing. This can be done at open conferences, as well as at more business intimate get-togethers of peers (the world's largest peer group for servicing regional directors operating in Central Eastern Europe, the Middle East and Africa is CEEMEA Business Group, for example; contact the author if you would like to join).

INTENSIFY MARKET MONITORING TO ANTICIPATE CHANGES AND PRIORITIZE RESOURCE ALLOCATIONS

As the global economy changes daily and impacts markets around the world with greater speed than ever before, it is crucial to improve the system for regular monitoring of markets. Despite fundamental stability of most emerging markets (see the previous chapter), currencies can fluctuate and growth can be patchy for reasons sometimes outside the control of well-run emerging market economies.

The whole exercise of market monitoring must have at least two goals. First, to determine which areas are likely to be growth markets in the upcoming period, why that is and then use that information to allocate business development resources to such places that deserve them. It is important that the whole "going deeper into emerging markets" exercise is executed in a sequence, starting from the most promising markets first. As most promising markets provide faster returns, it is easier to decide on deeper investments in those markets. The second goal is to determine and anticipate external economic risks that could derail otherwise solid business plans. Those executives that are able to inform their superiors about risks in advance are usually better able to protect their careers.

CONTINGENCY PLANNING AND CONTINGENCY EXECUTION ARE ESSENTIAL

Anyone with any meaningful experience in emerging markets has experienced something unexpected (or not well-anticipated) economically and politically. Sudden events, such as currency depreciations or sudden political changes, can have a major impact on corporate plans and budgets. This is why companies should nurture a culture of contingency planning in those markets where market monitoring suggests there are risks.

Most companies that I work with now have a plan B for at least their important markets. Such plans can include identifying which costs to cut quickly to protect profitability in case of a major currency depreciation; or which measures to implement to gain share when everyone else is in panic mode. In any case, plan Bs are also a useful career protection tool, because they are supposed to at least preserve market share targets or profitability targets during those periods when top line growth falls below budget. I advocate to all my clients that contingency planning on a country level should be institutionalized, since economic volatility will be with us for years to come (see my description of some key economic risks and why the global economy is quite nuts in the last chapter of my new short executive book, *Global Economy*).

Another thing I advocate is that firms must make sure they can really implement their contingency plans. It is all fine being able to put a plan B on paper, but the devil is in implementation. One of the regional directors of a major IT company says:

> "When the 'Arab Spring' revolutions started in the Middle East in early 2011, we had major problems with sales in markets such as Egypt and Tunisia. But because we are so deeply local and with extremely good

personal links to our local distributors/partners, I was able to go to our partners in Saudi Arabia and Turkey and ask them to order more from us than originally planned. While they did not like the idea initially, they did it only because they considered me a long-standing friend who needed help. So we increased our sales in Saudi and Turkey and compensated what we lost in Egypt and Tunisia. I met my budget for 2011."

This anecdote is just one of the many that confirm that contingency plans are so much easier to execute when firms are well established locally, with strong personal relationships with key stakeholders. In the end, very deep local presence is not only critical to build a sustainable business, but also to manage downturns (and there will be no shortage of temporary downturns in the future!).

MARKET SHARE IS AN IMPORTANT KPI

Most companies that I work with have recently elevated market share as a KPI (key performance indicator) to a prominent position in terms of how they evaluate their country and regional managers throughout emerging markets. This makes sense. While achieving sustainable revenue and profit growth is, of course, an overarching medium- to long-term goal, many executives are acutely aware that demand can be volatile in the short term for various reasons.

And when markets are hit economically, it is those firms that nurture and grow their market shares when times are tough that usually find it easier to grow sales and profits when good times return. There is enough historic evidence to suggest that firms with a stronger market share are finding it easier to feed their profit growth in the future, they are able to command prices, they find it easier to get rid of competitors who have lower shares by initiating temporary price wars, and of course, find it easier to retain and motivate staff who work for a winning company.

The other strategic reason for focusing on strong market shares relates to what I discussed earlier in this chapter. Namely, one of the key measurements for outperforming competition over an extended period of time is to grow market share. Therefore, market share gains are important strategically, operationally, in the short term and the long term, and in every part of the segmentation pyramid (more on this in the next chapter).

CONSIDER ACQUISITIONS AS A WAY TO GROW

Building sustainable business structures for organic growth is an essential part of future success in emerging markets, but acquisitions should be part of the growth mix. Organic growth is sometimes hard to find in certain geographies due to volatile economies and tough competition. Also, organic growth often does not meet the very ambitious growth targets that some firms set for themselves. Acquisitions can be a good solution for adding extra growth. To meet such ambitious growth targets, a growing number of international firms are creating teams that *proactively* seek out acquisition targets around the world.

But companies must make sure they do not end up among those firms that fail to reach their acquisition goals, or even end up in trouble after an acquisition is completed. I noticed over the years that acquisitions in emerging markets fail more often than not. And usually they fail for two underlying reasons: a badly understood and executed due diligence process and a badly understood and executed post-acquisition restructuring/integration.

The failure rate of acquisitions is actually higher in emerging markets than it is in the developed world, mainly because it is sometimes very difficult to make assumptions about future earnings streams and to fully understand targets. The number of things that can go wrong during the due diligence process is frighteningly long and I look at those items later in the chapter on acquisitions.

BE EXTRAORDINARILY CAREFUL WITH COST-CUTTING IN GROWTH MARKETS

As developed markets struggle, many firms are in some sort of cost-cutting mode. Sadly, this mode often also affects markets that are clearly in a growth mode in terms of GDP growth, current sales growth and most importantly, growth potential. Of course, it is understandable that some CEOs – under intense sales, profit or shareholder pressures at home – decide to cut costs globally. Sometimes, the pressures are such that short-term concerns become overwhelming.

I always urge caution when it comes to cost cutting in emerging markets. First, most companies report that they are still underinvested in most markets and if they would add more resources, there would most likely be more growth. Second, companies have to be careful that cost cutting does not affect face-to-face functions, relationships, market shares and growth initiatives. Third, be sensitive to any pull-outs from the markets – locals remember those who come and go, and rebuilding lost relationships or market share could take a painfully long time. Rebuilding lost market share or relationships can also be extraordinarily expensive and in the worst case, some firms are unable to rebuild them at all – in other words, loss of market position can become permanent as competitors plug the customer or geographic gaps.

And finally, over the years it has become clear that those firms that cut costs excessively in their emerging market operations are simply left without the necessary resources to invest in new sources of sales growth. This, needless to say, is a disaster for any firm that is thinking about building a sustainable business model.

AVOID JOINT VENTURES IF YOU CAN; OR STRUCTURE THEM IN A WAY TO PROTECT YOUR FUTURE

It is hard to generalize and there are many firms that run successful joint ventures in emerging markets, but the majority of joint ventures have either failed miserably, or took an enormous amount of time to dismantle (and firms lost share in the meantime), or were in the end converted by multinationals into majority or full ownership. Joint ventures (JVs) are not easy to run, even in multinationals' domestic or well-understood markets, and they are even more difficult to run in complicated, culturally different, emerging markets.

The number of things that can go wrong are endless. Companies have experienced problems in the areas of strategic differences about the future of the business, financial disagreements, cultural disagreements, and lack of trust. In the worst cases, local partners have set up a parallel business and have channeled revenues there instead of into the established joint venture.

Many firms consider joint ventures as a form of market entry or market expansion, and usually the main consideration is that it is a cheaper market entry option. But I am convinced that entering emerging markets on the cheap is simply not good enough anymore to create business success. Competitive pressures are so intense, and will get even more intense in the future, that only firms that are deeply entrenched in local markets, with strong control over their business (sales and marketing at a minimum), will be able to gain share.

Of course it is understandable if certain legislations require joint venture creations. There are sectors and areas – for example in China, India or some Gulf markets – where joint ventures are simply required or highly recommended. In such cases, there is no real choice but to set them up and to try to run them by using best practices for running joint ventures. Or make sure that the contracts (if legally possible) allow companies to take control eventually, or at least exit the contracts without too much pain.

If there is no legal requirement, companies should ask themselves before going into a potential joint venture nightmare the following question: what is it that the local partner can bring us that we cannot do ourselves? And if the decision is made to go the JV route, then it is useful to have some effective exit clauses or potentially an option to buy the local partner at a certain price or price range. There are many good examples of firms going into

JVs with a buyout option. First, they use the JV period to assess the market and staff in the local partner; then, when the time comes for bigger expansion (and the local partner can't afford it), they look to takeover. This can work well, but negotiating a buyout clause is not always easy.

THINK OF STEP-UP CHANGES

If our sales in emerging markets are 100, how do we step up the effort to hit 200 or even 300 in three to four years? What resources do we need to achieve this kind of growth? Do we need to replace some of our internal "dead wood" staff that block growth initiatives because of their own comfort or complacency? Do we need to replace some of our distributors who seem to be "sleeping at the wheel"? How much more do we need to invest in our own staff and in marketing/sales to achieve fast growth?

These are the types of questions that many firms are asking themselves these days. These are good questions to ask because once companies do a thorough analysis of countries, business potential, and opportunities missed so far, they inevitably conclude that there is more space for growth than conventional wisdom would allow. This whole process is about challenging that wisdom and trying to energize the teams around the world to think creatively about how to step up the push for growth.

"Step up change" is a worthy effort but I find that it is often badly executed. In a recent example, one of the consumer goods firms that I know very well has carried out "step up" change exercises. But when it came to implementation, they replaced some distributors, a few internal executives (without actually trying to engage them, and by losing them they lost key relationships and experience), and then forgot the crucial thing – every step up effort in emerging markets has to be matched by an equivalent increase in upfront investment in local infrastructure and people, and of course sales, marketing and brand-building.

Ironically, firms often find that the new distributors or staff are no better than the ones they replaced. (Often, they are even worse.) Sometimes, it is not about who the distributor or staff are, but finding a way of working with them (more on that in the later chapters on marketing and HR excellence).

AVOID DOING THINGS THAT MIGHT DAMAGE YOUR LONG-TERM BUSINESS

Consider the following points:
- Did you support your distributor during difficult times?
- Did you raise prices so sharply after a depreciation that you lost market share but preserved short-term profitability?
- Did you stop spending on marketing and promotion when times were tough, despite the fact that business history shows that companies that overspend their competitors during crises always win long term?
- Did you cut costs so savagely in some markets that you lost share and relationships?

RECOGNIZE AND APPRECIATE THAT DIFFERENT MARKETS SOMETIMES REQUIRE DIFFERENT APPROACHES TO BUILDING BUSINESS

Companies should proactively move from a one-size-fits-all emerging markets strategy or one-size-fits-all regional strategies for the Middle East, Africa or Latin America. The strategic "devil" is in *country* level detail and companies that get this wrong will find it hard to compete in the future.

RECOGNIZE AND APPRECIATE THAT DIFFERENT MARKETS SOMETIMES REQUIRE DIFFERENT TIMEFRAMES FOR SUCCESS

Anyone who has had a chance to visit a wide range of countries for business knows that time is not viewed in the same way everywhere. Things can sometimes happen so slowly in some countries that it does come as a culture shock to many who are used to a fast-paced approach. The truth is that most companies often underestimate how long it will take to do work in certain countries. And if the time involved is underestimated, so is the cost. And then because the costs are higher than expected, some companies get cold feet about certain growth initiatives and upfront investment.

This is why it is tremendously important to appreciate that the time involved in doing certain things (even mundane administrative items) often far exceeds that of the developed world. Country level and regional directors are usually very aware of this, but the trick is to make sure that the people in global headquarters also understand this before specific growth initiatives are put in place. Sometimes, initiatives can be delayed so much or miss internal deadlines that the competency of country directors are, wrongly, put in to question.

Alternatively, the funny thing is that sometimes, things happen faster than in the developed world. One of my largest clients told me the following story:

> "We were about to open a new manufacturing site in mainland China and found a good piece of land. We invited the local developer to start talking about the project. It was 8 a.m. Once he briefly heard what we wanted, he phoned someone and within one hour someone else showed up, whom he introduced as an architect. They spoke quickly and the "architect" put sketches and drawings together while the developer spoke. After 20 minutes, the architect was on the phone and within one hour there were six earth-moving pieces of equipment on site and they started to dig. And then the developer said that the building would be finished in less than a week. No permits. No paperwork. Nothing. This is when we had to tell him to stop right there, because we wanted to do everything properly. He still insisted that you do paperwork later and that there was nothing to worry about. We did not go along with his plan, but once the paperwork was done – which was quick – we were up and running with the new plant in record time, by any global standard."

DO NOT MICRO MANAGE FROM A DISTANCE

"I had a telephone conversation with my boss for 25 minutes arguing why two of my star sales people required an above average pay rise. And I am responsible for one of the fastest growing emerging markets in the world," said one executive in charge of the Turkish market. Another one said: "The list of things I have to seek approval for is endless. Nominally, I am in charge of this sub-regional cluster, but in reality it is run by control freaks and bean counters in our EMEA headquarters." These are the typical executive complaints I hear in interactions with regional and country level executives. Ex-CEO of Tesco Terry Leahy once said: "We realize now that micro-managing from a distance does not work."

For lasting success in emerging markets, companies must give their country and regional directors a sense of business ownership for the territory they are responsible for. Obviously, you do not want to create country-level kingdoms and you want to preserve corporate identity, KPI reporting and integrity, but it is important to allow local offices to take charge of the business on the ground.

MOVE MANUFACTURING AND R&D TO CHEAPER LOCATIONS

In order to succeed against fast-rising competitive pressures, it is essential that companies look very carefully at the entire cost equation when it comes to product development and product manufacturing. Getting this right in the next decade will be more important than it was in the last decade. The vast majority of multinational companies I deal with already manufacture outside their home markets (and plan to increase this further), and those that do not are planning to do so.

There are several conclusions to be drawn based on past corporate successes and failures.
- First, companies have found out that setting up greenfield manufacturing sites tends to be easier than acquiring existing ones or going into some joint ventures. In other words, companies should be careful before deciding on an acquisition or a joint venture route.
- Second, take your time choosing the right country and the right location within a country. Spend time looking at the infrastructure, the experiences of other firms, availability of suppliers, availability of free trade agreements, labour costs and availability, ability to operate 7 days per week, 24 hours per day, frequency of strikes, labour laws, availability and price of land and utilities, etc.
- Third, do extensive tax and incentive shopping tours before you pick the country or a location within a country. Check the availability and practicalities of any special economic zones.
- Fourth, do not ignore political risks. I am usually relatively relaxed about political risks when it comes to developing sales, but when you need to invest US $50 million, $100 million or $200 million in a manufacturing plant, you had better do it in a location where the risk of some political blow up or interference is virtually non-existent. (Of course, if you just use the manufacturing site to produce for the country in question and the country is huge, like Nigeria or China, then you might have to take that risk.)
- Fifth, consider outsourcing manufacturing, but make sure you don't end up in some public relations disaster if some investigative journalist finds out that your goods are being

made by kids or labourers who are not allowed to take a toilet break. Make sure you control and monitor those outsourced manufacturing plants properly (not just visits from a distance, but by placing your own supervisors within the factories).
- Sixth, make sure you check you do not miss any "brownfield" sites, such as existing abandoned buildings with the right infrastructure connections, which could quickly be converted into a functioning manufacturing site. These things could save time and money.

There is a very visible trend of moving research and development into faster-growing markets. This is increasingly being done for at least two reasons. First, many firms are in the game of "downward innovation" and trying to develop products below the premium segment (see Chapter 3 for a discussion on marketing excellence). This is usually better and more cheaply done in cheaper locations, where local researchers will be better placed to understand the needs of local consumers and customers. Second, even some high-end research is being carried out in cheaper locations purely for cost reasons. Scientists in Russia or China do not cost as much as those in Chicago or Frankfurt.

But when it comes to moving R&D to locations in emerging markets, companies must ensure they try and protect their intellectual property as much as possible. Most companies place only parts of their research into a country. Only headquarters get the whole picture and know the final product. This careful approach can surely buy at least some time in the market place and ensure a good start. Most products will inevitably be copied anyway and most executives today believe there is no such thing as full intellectual property protection.

MAKE SURE YOU DO NOT UNDER-PENETRATE MARKETS

Find out how much average multinationals sell in certain geographies as a percentage of their global sales and you will have a rough, but telling, indicator of your own market penetration. If you are close to the average penetration of others, you know that you have invested roughly as much as others. But if you are substantially below this figure, it is worth spending time understanding why that is.

My long-standing experience shows that companies have below-average market penetration (in terms of sales as a percentage of global sales) due to lack of upfront investment and sustained brand-building. Surveys show that Latin America usually accounts for 6% of global sales, the same figure for Central Eastern Europe, while the Middle East and North Africa account for 3% of global sales, emerging Asia 14–15% and Sub-Saharan Africa 1–1.5%. In other words, reasonably well-established multinationals should generate about 35% of their overall sales in emerging geographies. Those who are below this percentage are underinvested; those who are above are doing well and moving in the right direction. The percentage of sales coming out of emerging markets will surely grow over the years, simply because economic and demographic growth will be faster.

INCREASE CULTURAL SENSITIVITY IN EVERYTHING YOU DO

Anyone who has ever done any sort of business in emerging markets has a horrible or funny anecdote to tell about how a company messed up by doing something culturally insensitive. One senior executive in the aerospace industry said: "There is nothing wrong with our guys in the headquarters, except they think they are the smartest and the world should bend to our views and rules." The mistakes linked to cultural insensitivities could have been forgiven 20 years ago. They could be understood 10 years ago. They could have been corrected even five years ago. Today, any such mistake carries a price tag.

Companies should be careful about many aspects of culture, including how they deal with people, designing and selling products that fit the culture, negotiating with partners, and dealing with government officials. No company can afford the negative consequences of cultural insensitivities any more – the amount of money spent on training junior to senior managers is increasing exponentially, especially in firms that are known for shipping employees to various locations around the world.

GET YOUR HR STRATEGY RIGHT

See Chapter 4, which covers key HR issues in emerging markets.

MOVE INNOVATION TO A COMPLETELY NEW LEVEL

See the next chapter, which deals with marketing excellence.

Chapter 3

BUILDING AND EXECUTING MARKETING EXCELLENCE

Product is everything.

—Steve Jobs

You miss 100% of the shots you never take.

— Wayne Gretzky

SO MUCH SUCCESS IN EMERGING markets depends on building and executing marketing excellence, that the topic deserves a chapter on its own. If the previous chapter was largely about building strategic and structural foundations, this one is about adding one of the critical elements on top of that foundation. This chapter examines what companies need to do with their product, distribution, promotion and pricing in order to build a sustainable business and to outperform competition in emerging markets.

PRODUCT
RETHINKING INNOVATION

Typical multinational firms have traditionally made money in the premium segment of the market and in many countries have reached enviable market positions with such products. All of them continue to innovate and create new premium products, to find new sources of sales growth or to gain market share. And this innovation at the premium level should continue to be an essential building block of future corporate success.

But as competition intensifies to new levels in emerging markets, then so should corporate innovation. For many of my clients it is now glaringly obvious that most international business battles will be won over the medium and long term by companies that compete in multiple market segments. And yet a number of companies still refuse to look beyond their traditional premium segment. This is fine if that is the global strategy. "We do not want to spend any time outside of the premium area and that is our deliberate strategy. We know we miss many growth opportunities with this approach but this is what we decided," said one regional director of an alcoholic drinks company I work with. If that is the case, that is fine, as long as the company is actually conscious it could be growing faster, but chooses to stay in a relatively narrow and busy premium market segment.

For many firms, developing products for more than one market/price segment has become an essential part of current and future success in emerging markets. We will all witness a growing number of firms launching more and more products in the second, third and lower segments of the segmentation pyramid in the next few years. I see many companies planning to execute this with more strength than ever before. Why is it strategically important to have a systematic and sustainable innovation strategy that looks beyond the traditional premium segment?

a) **Growth potential.** Companies that compete in second, third or lower market segments will find that significant sales growth will actually come from that space in the next decade (and beyond) in emerging markets. Taken as a whole, the biggest sales growth potential will ultimately be in emerging markets, and within them, in all segments below premium. Many firms are particularly keen on developing products for the middle of the segmentation pyramid.

b) **Competitive pressures from multinationals.** Even multinationals that refused to move below the traditional premium segment are now at least discussing the issue seriously. Goods and services from all sectors are now in this game, or will be very soon. Firms realize that if they leave the second or third tier of the market to competitors, they are endangering their strategic positions for the medium and long term and losing overall market share and growth in the short term.

c) **Competitive pressures from emerging market multinationals.** They usually start at the low end of the segmentation pyramid, but in recent years emerging market multinationals have been moving upwards, attacking middle segments. Some have already ventured into premium areas, or are about to do so. Many firms realize they have to either compete head on or buy these companies before they become too big and too expensive to buy.

d) **Developing products and services for multiple segments is not just a strategic issue for emerging markets.** It is also relevant for the developed world, where companies of all sizes and households will all be more price sensitive in the new age of moderate and low economic growth (see Chapter 1).

e) **In the new age of moderation, more consumers will be trading downwards** (just as many have done during the last few years). Historical case studies show that once a customer moves down and is reasonably satisfied with a "good enough" product, it is hard to move him up again. The danger for multinationals that rely just on the premium segment is that they might lose many customers that could be incredibly difficult to lure back into the premium segment again. Why would you want to surrender those sales to competitors? It is better if a consumer down-trades to your product, rather than a competitors' product. At least, you keep the relationship and it will be easier to move them up again.

Many companies that I work with have already started to compete in multiple market segments, although most shy away from the bottom of the pyramid, which is a game on its own and extraordinarily difficult to implement. But focusing on the second and third tier of the market is something companies are learning how to handle. And it is far from easy. There are legitimate concerns about the cannibalization of existing premium products and margins. Many firms have delayed their decisions to go in this direction for a long time, but it is now clear that you either do it, or you surrender a chunk of the market to someone else. It is a strategic choice that has an impact on the future growth potential of any firm. It is a strategic choice that each firm has to make.

Multiple market segments

My advice to companies is that the future will be won by those firms that have products that can serve multiple market needs and that focus on gaining share in those segments. While venturing into some of the lower segments can indeed jeopardize overall margins, it is crucially important from a strategic point of view. It weakens competition, it generates new sales growth in segments that were previously untouched, it builds market positions for the long term, it works with consumers and customers who aspire to premium products but can't afford them now – and it prepares the ground for future up-selling. In the end, it serves the ultimate purpose, which is to outperform the competition and build a sustainable business for the future.

Competing in multiple market segments is a necessity but it is not easy to implement. Some companies liken it to "creating a company within a company". Many things have to change to be able to produce and market a product in, for example, the second tier. Companies have to rethink where and how they do R&D, where and how they manufacture, where they source raw materials and components, how they organize their entire supply chain, and how they approach the customer/consumer.

To create "downward" or "affordable" or "strip down" innovation, firms are increasingly moving their R&D to emerging markets. The shift of manufacturing to cheaper locations is also ongoing. Marketing cannot use the same messaging as it does for premium products. All in all, to make it work, there has to be full support from the very top of the corporate hierarchy. And everyone should understand that this is not an easy change to implement. It is a big strategic leap but the one that will ensure long-standing success and survival.

At the same time, companies should not forget that innovating upwards (or creating new exciting premium products) remains as important as ever. In addition, companies should be aware that there is a great opportunity for launching and selling super premium goods and services in emerging markets to the narrow segment of the very wealthy (or those wanting to appear wealthy – and there are so many of those in emerging markets!). And last, but not least, a lot of firms are now innovating and building different sub segments under the overall premium label. New smart phones from Nokia (the smart phone being a premium item) have different price points and some technological differences. BMW cars are all premium but in different price segments (from small to large cars).

If headquarters are reluctant to go into lower market segments, regional directors are using three approaches to convince them. First, regional directors of all emerging regions join forces to argue the case, because they all need products for a variety of segments to grow in the future. Second, they take the CEO and top corporate officers to talk to customers in emerging markets, so they can themselves see the market needs, price points and competition. Third, they argue that products and services in lower segments will also do well in the increasingly price-sensitive developed world. Therefore, serving multiple market segments is not just a part of an emerging markets strategy, but also part of a global strategy. Once CEOs and top officers realize this, it is easier to start moving the whole company in this direction.

Serving multiple market segments is not just a part of an emerging markets strategy, but also part of a global strategy.

One word of caution based on some recent unhappy experiences. Several companies I know well had launched products in the second and third tiers in the market but then did not really invest in building those brands over the last few years. They declared the initiative a failure and withdrew. The regional guys in charge were keen to support the newly launched brands but could not get enough resources. "Now it will take at least a decade until we do this again because there will always be someone up there who will remember how we 'failed'. The truth is we did not fail with the product and the intention, but our execution and brand-building was incredibly half-hearted." It is therefore essential that companies understand that launching products in new segments will fail if not properly and continuously supported and if there is no clear brand differentiation.

The speed of innovation matters, too. One of the senior executives from a medical devices firm I have been working with for several years said that:

> "…70% of our growth in emerging markets currently comes from products we launched in the last two years. This is the only way we can stay competitive against old and new competitors. At the same time, we position those older, replaced, products as second tier. In fact we are not doing any innovation downwards. By improving our premium, our older products naturally fall into that second category for a while until they are replaced, too."

I think the overall message about innovation for the future in emerging markets can be broken down as follows:
- it has to be focused on multiple segments;
- it must nurture and improve premium;
- it must think about super premium; and it has move faster and more creatively than ever before.

It also must be in constant tune with changing consumer and customer needs in every market.

Treat customers/consumers with respect

Another item for the future is that one should never underestimate local consumers and customers. A frequent mistake that I have observed is that some companies have tried to "cheat" their way into emerging markets by launching products that were discontinued in the developed world. This was always a questionable strategy and often backfired, but now it has no chance of success unless some of these older products are deliberately targeting lower segments of the market. Despite their relative poverty, many emerging markets consumers and customers are extremely well-informed about new technologies, new products and in the words of one my clients, "…know exactly when someone wants to sell them shit wrapped up in nice packaging."

Companies that keep innovating during economic slowdowns come out stronger when outlooks brighten. If you do not have a product or service for a newly identified market need, start an internal initiative to develop and launch new products for multiple market segments. Sometimes, just small adjustments of the existing products and repositioning of new brands can work, too.

Innovation through customers in emerging markets must become institutionalized in every serious firm.

Increasingly, many firms innovate through their local customers and consumers. Of course, firms continue to invent products that consumers and customers "did not even know they needed", and this is a good thing. At the same time, by increasing the frequency of conversations with local customers and consumers, many firms are giving their R&D teams important customer/consumer feedback. Like a lot of things in international business today, even innovation is thus becoming a very localized affair, taking into account the views of the local final buyers. Innovation through customers in emerging markets must become institutionalized in every serious firm.

Today, changes are happening within the corporate teams responsible for innovation. First, CEOs are getting involved themselves and are trying to involve local offices and cross-functional teams to play the game and provide feedback. Second, the traditional four innovation categories – revolutionary, evolutionary, differentiating and fast-fail innovation – are also getting different allocations. Companies that have traditionally invested only 10–15% of total R&D spending in revolutionary innovation are now increasing this percentage. This is because everyone is keen on creating game-changing products, regardless of the segment.

Several companies I work with have recently launched a number of newly-created product categories. Some of these were original and therefore opened up a completely new growth space. Some were bundles of existing products and services, where smart bundling created a market advantage. One senior executive from an Italian food company said recently:

> "We are masters of inventing products that no one has ever come up with before. This fact by itself excites consumers and most of our new product launches succeed in emerging markets. We find that consumers there are very open to new ideas, to something very cool. They will shift from a brand they know to a completely new one in minutes and this is why we are so focused on creating our own growth patterns through innovation."

ENGAGE IN A VERY SCIENTIFIC, FREQUENT AND LOCALIZED UNDERSTANDING OF CUSTOMER GROUPS AND SEGMENTS

Companies have always been engaged in understanding market segments and their customers/consumers. But there are three things that are now being done to ensure long-standing success in emerging markets. First, research should be carried out more frequently, because economic volatility can quickly shift consumer/customer preferences and behaviour. Second, research is more locally focused on specific countries than ever. In the past, too many firms have been putting their regional research results together in joint graphs and slides. This is not enough anymore. Third, research itself is becoming more sophisticated and more scientific.

I still find it surprising to observe how many firms continue to sell their products based on research they did two or three years ago. This is simply not enough anymore. A tough and ever-changing economic environment is constantly creating new consumer/customer preferences and new needs. Also, a lot of the research that I see in corporate meetings is regionalized under broader EMEA, Americas, or Asia Pacific umbrellas, without enough depth given to local markets. It is understandable when medium-sized firms do not want to spend money on such frequent localized research, but for multinationals there is really no excuse (if they want to be important or dominant players). The cost of doing such research is relatively low compared to the benefits it can bring in terms of rebuilding a product portfolio, smarter positioning and smarter marketing messaging that resonates with buyers.

Astonishingly, one of the largest consumer goods firms in the world recently told me two things that looked like an exaggeration, but the regional director was serious: "After the crisis, we really do not know much about our buyers. And we assume they might have changed beyond recognition." Because of these assumptions, this company has launched a multi-million dollar research project in all countries around the world to find out what the post-crisis consumer really wants, how he/she thinks, etc. When the research results came in, there were many surprises: these clearly showed, for example, the need to extend a product's portfolio both up and down the segmentation pyramid. It also showed that the positioning of certain products was completely wrong.

In the light of this new focus on multiple market segments, companies are questioning how many market segments they could potentially serve in each country. They dig deeper into each segment to find out what the actual market needs and the potential price point of each element. There is a consensus view that more growth in the future ought to come from the middle of the pyramid. Customers have changed in the post-crisis world and companies need to find out how they've changed. As the regional head of an IT company said:

> "Once we started looking at small and medium-sized local firms, we realized that there is a massive market for us out there and we are now trying to address this with major product changes and by adjusting some of the existing products to those needs."

The ultimate goal of the above exercise is to be in constant tune with changing market needs – and then to do something about it.

TO FIND MORE GROWTH, MATCH THE PRODUCT'S PORTFOLIO WITH ACTUAL NEEDS

As research tracks the market's needs as they evolve in each country, there is one exercise all firms should embrace as part of an ongoing strategy for the future. That is to match the product or services portfolio with these evolving and sometimes fast-changing needs. This means that many firms will have to extend their product portfolio into new directions and new segments either through organic growth (via innovation) or through acquisitions. Many are currently seeking ways to create product extensions and new product categories in which competitive pressures are not as intense.

Other firms will seek to attack new market segments with the same product. One executive from the drinks industry said to me recently:

> "Our energy drinks have traditionally targeted the young. For years we did not think there would be much interest among adults or even pensioners. Several pilots we did showed there was ample opportunity to extend the same product to completely new groups of buyers. When we finally started doing it, we faced some challenges initially, but overall the approach has been a success. We were weighing up if it made sense to sell our premium product to more age groups or to launch secondary cheaper brands. We opted for the first and it works well – and we are now going to do it globally."

SEEK TO QUICKLY MATCH YOUR COMPETITORS' PRODUCT AND POSITIONING STRATEGY – OR BETTER, LEAD THE WAY

If a competitor launches something completely innovative that suddenly starts to take market share, be sure you match it with your own product in as many emerging markets as possible. The reason why this is so important in emerging markets is that buyers are still fickle in many places – brand loyalties are not as entrenched as they are in the US or Japan. So a new product launch can quickly change the market share landscape. Of course in an ideal world, each company will want to lead the way with game-changing products. But if it happens that competitors are faster, each company must have the ability to quickly organize a task force to match it. The last thing one should allow is for a competitor to enjoy some quiet time with a new launch.

EMERGING MARKETS OFFER OPPORTUNITIES FOR NEW POSITIONING – USE THEM TO IMPROVE MARGINS

Since many brands are not well known in new markets around the world, companies have an opportunity to position their products differently than in home markets. Many firms have actually opted for positioning them higher on the segmentation pyramid. From jeans to alcohol, food to car brands, it is happening in many segments. This usually involves taking a product that is seen as middle of the pyramid in Germany or the US and positioning it as a premium product in South Africa or India.

PROMOTION
KEEP SPENDING ON ALL ASPECTS OF BRAND-BUILDING AND SUSTAIN IT

There is enough historical evidence demonstrating that firms that outspend competitors on various brand-building exercises (especially during challenging economic times) tend also to outperform them. This is usually first reflected in market share gains, but stronger market share positions carry a number of medium to long-term advantages with them. Yet, this is often forgotten by many firms operating in emerging markets.

Even when economic times are relatively good, many multinationals and new emerging players are cautious with marketing spend and tend to rely on their distributors to somehow build the business for them, or instead of them. The reliance on the supposed global strength of certain brands is often the reason why companies are reluctant to spend too much "on brands that everybody knows". Perhaps multinationals could get away with this attitude in the past, but those days are long gone.

Only firms that are smart, overwhelming and consistent investors in their brands will outperform fast-rising competition in emerging markets in the future. It is simply not possible anymore to build and sustain market positions in emerging markets without that committed spending.

> "Internally we call it 'consistency of spending' on our brands. That's what this is all about. This is important in developed markets for the future, but it is even more critical in emerging markets, because loyalties do not run deep and we need to keep reminding our buyers about our products, what they are, what they stand for, how to use them, etc, etc. It is a never-ending commitment that is not cheap, but we do not see any other way forward," said an executive in the consumer goods industry.

This point is equally important during tough economic times. Firms gain share whenever they outspend competitors during economic downturns. And those firms that gain share when times are tough always do well (especially at the bottom line) when good times return. A good dose of corporate long-termism is needed to implement this. Some recent examples of this come from Central and Eastern Europe, which has been going through a rough economic patch over the last few years.

A good client of mine offers a good illustration of the challenge faced by firms during times of slow economic growth:

> "Me and my colleagues on the ground have recognized this period as a time when it is indeed possible to build shares in a few market segments in which we operate. Some of our competitors are pulling out, some are disappearing and the market has opened up for anyone aggressive enough to take share. However, because our profits are stagnant, we are unable to get the approval from HQ to bring marketing spend to where it should be – that is, higher than our competitors. At the same time, our CEO has just bragged about the company sitting on record amounts of cash with which nothing is being done at the moment – but it is good for the share price and people who have massive stock options. It is a short-term view that prevents us from dominating emerging markets. What a shame. I have basically given up trying to convince them."

Another executive active in Latin America says:

> "We had yet another round of some international cash outflow from our key markets and currencies depreciated for no obvious reason. In the past, when

something like this happened, we always stopped spending for some time to assess the impact on profitability. Today, we just keep doing the same thing as if nothing has happened. We cannot afford to lose share. We know the currencies will bounce back fairly quickly. In fact, our internal mindset has changed so much that we now almost cherish the short windows when there is market turmoil. We see them as short-lived opportunities to increase share at the expense of competitors, who will go into a knee-jerk reaction of stopping promotions or even pulling out. Don't get me wrong, we do not wish frequent currency depreciations, but we know how to handle it now."

MAKE SURE YOUR PROMOTION ACTIVITIES ARE NOT LAZY

Do you belong to a company that takes centrally created ads (global or regional) and then uses them to promote products and services in countries around the world? Do you belong to a company whose local websites are not 100% translated into local languages but merely provide links to the master website? If you do, you should look to change sooner rather than later. More and more companies are moving in the direction of localizing most of their promotional activities.

One of my large clients in the consumer business has completely reworked their promotional campaigns in the CEE and MEA regions, and are now rolling out similar programs in emerging Asia and Latin America. Previously they had a regional approach using TV, print and other ads. Their regional marketing director reported:

"When I was brought in to revamp marketing in the firm, I wanted to make sure that our ads really reached people and that marketing messages resonated. We were losing some share in most markets. It was not alarming, but the decline was steady and worrying. Then, after another round of marketing research, it was clear that ads were not resonating and touching the consumer. TV ads were simply dubbed in the local language, but with anonymous faces and nothing local to connect with buyers. We now run separate campaigns for each country. We found that in each market people cared about different things. We are using recognizable local faces as our product ambassadors. Over the last 18 months, ever since our marketing went from being globally/regionally lazy to locally focused, we have gained between 7–18% market share points, depending on the market. We are now going to the next stage and the pilot campaigns are showing fantastic results. The pilots in three countries showed that when we focused on provincial cultural differences and included provincial humour, we gained even more share. So we are moving even deeper into each market. Country level is not enough. The future will be much more granular and scientific, not only in terms of regions within countries, but also understanding market segments in each region and province. This costs money but the returns are great, even in the short term. It is worth every penny spent."

ENGAGE A BROADER TEAM TO FINE-TUNE MESSAGES THAT RESONATE

Many companies that I have observed in recent years are very keen on standing out from the competition when it comes to connecting with the buyers. It sounds like a cliché, but there are so many firms that readily admit they operate in the same old pattern year after year.

> "When we look at how to find more buyers and how to reach them with a message that makes them think about us, we never leave that exercise to the marketing team alone. The team that looks at this is highly cross-fertilized. We learned that good ideas can be hiding in other divisions. At the last meeting, two fabulous ideas came from a young finance manager and from an about to retire engineer. In addition to having all divisions participate, we also want to make sure that we have various age groups in the team. I like to have really young team members who will look at things very differently, but also very old ones like me, who will remember some good things from the past or have an alternative angle," says the regional director of a large industrial company.

DISTRIBUTION

One of the most critical success factors is in making the product available to every potential customer and to control the whole process well, either directly or via local distributors (or through a combination of both). Despite the need and ongoing drive to deepen local presence in as many emerging markets as possible, most companies continue to work with their local distributors. The level of involvement still ranges from having distributors run almost everything on the ground (a strategy I earlier described as clearly not sufficient) to just running the physical distribution of products (where multinationals have taken direct control over importing). The latter approach, of course, is not cheap but the benefits can outweigh the cost, sometimes even in small countries.

The underlying key to success is to have a strong working relationship with distributors, where the multinational supports the distributor with its own sales and marketing staff on the ground, as well as with other forms of support (see below). Companies that elect to leave distributors in charge of markets and brand-building usually fail to outperform the competition or build sustainable positions in emerging markets.

A well-functioning, well-capitalized and proactive distributor is a wonderful addition to the organization. But no distributor can work well over an extended period of time without close supervision and control. Eventually, a mismatch between corporate and distributor ambitions will start creating strains in the relationship and become an obstacle to faster growth. There are many critical factors to consider when preparing to work with a distributor. Below is a selection of some important items that were frequently mentioned by executives during my research for this book.

PARTNER SELECTION – SELECT THOSE THAT ARE WILLING AND ABLE TO FOLLOW YOUR FAST-GROWTH STRATEGY

If there is one mantra that I hear time and time again from seasoned executives, it is that the most important thing is to "find the right partner". The right partner can make or break the business. What are the criteria that determine the suitability of a partner? Executives cite things such as having enough capital to buy enough products and enable expansion; professional and knowledgeable staff; the right infrastructure in terms of warehouses and logistics; an IT system that can be linked to multinationals; sector expertise; good relationships with retailers or groups of final buyers; and the ability to provide customer and after-sales services and the nationwide reach or desire/financial capability to do so.

There is increasingly one criterion that companies often prioritize above all others and which will continue to be important in the future. This is the willingness of the distributor (read: owner) to embrace the growth strategy of the multinational and to proactively contribute to it. A growing number of multinationals find that their existing distributors (as a rule already relatively well-off individuals) are not necessarily keen on following new ultra-fast growth strategies that companies are trying to put in place in high growth markets. Sometimes, distributors are simply financially too weak to follow fast growth strategies. Consequently, one of the key criteria for selecting new distributors involves assessing their pro-growth attitude and the ability to finance and execute it.

Companies are using a multitude of ways to select new distributors, including word-of-mouth recommendations, observing who distributes competitors or non-competitors products, or sometimes, just advertising in the local media. But the real job is in making sure that selected candidates meet internal corporate criteria. Companies are visiting distributors' offices and other facilities, interviewing owners and staff, doing investigative checks about the company regarding their finances or compliance issues, interviewing retailers and other final buyers, testing knowledge and expertise, and looking for evidence of track record of growth.

I always tell my clients to be extraordinarily careful when selecting a distributor, and to invest enough time and money in the search for the "right" partner. It is better not to rush into relationships without first making thorough checks. Some relationships are difficult to unwind, especially in some complex jurisdictions, for example in the Middle East (I have a whole bunch of clients in courts throughout the Gulf trying to extract themselves from old distributor contracts).

Before the selection is made, it is also incredibly important to understand the history of the distributor. Does he have a tendency to quickly switch from one company to another, or from one type of product to another? Is he in the business short term to make a quick buck with whoever offers the best deal this year? These days, companies can ill-afford to end up with distributors who are even more short-termist than some of the multinationals. Loyalty matters, and it is important to check their loyalty track record.

Companies should also make it clear what the key corporate guidelines will be in terms of pricing, brand-building, services or any other feature of the business that will ensure the smooth running of the operation. Companies are increasingly telling potential distributors: "If we choose you, these are things we will include in the contract. If you don't like it, let's not waste each other's time." And in addition to communicating in advance corporate guidelines that will define the future relationship, companies must ensure that potential partners are familiar with the long-term strategic goals of the multinational company.

WORKING WITH DISTRIBUTORS – SOME IMPORTANT POINTS

To compete against future multiple competitive threats in sometimes volatile economies, it is essential to ensure more control over the business, and this includes making sure distributors are integrated into multinational companies. That usually means that companies should open as many offices around the world as possible – even small "one man and a dog"-type offices in small countries are better than letting local distributors take full charge. Controlling the business from a distance is a thing of the past and insufficient in today's business environment. Ideally, in representative offices or subsidiaries, multinationals should make sure that enough marketing and sales staff are on the ground to build brands and work actively with local distributors and other partners.

Local placements within distributor organization

More and more companies put some of their own staff to physically work in local distributors' offices, to make sure that business is run well day-to-day to the benefit of the multinational. This is sometimes also a way to put someone on the ground if a company does not want to invest in a "one man and a dog office". This is also important because some distributors often work for more companies than one and closer control ensures your company and brands get enough focus and attention. Companies are also making sure that there is at least one person in the distributor organization that represents their interests exclusively. This is usually done through so-called "key person clauses" in distributor contracts.

Building strong relationships

It is important that country and also regional leaders build strong personal relationships with distributors. Companies recognize this and this is why so many regional directors are trying to increase local presence in so many high growth markets. This is important regardless of the economic climate. In good times, it helps drive the business and in bad times, it helps execute contingency plans. But such relationships cannot be developed properly without deep local presence and senior management continuity. Local partners must feel a part of the organization and be able see the lucrative road ahead. Companies increasingly understand that building these relationships is not an overnight exercise. It requires time, money and excellent interpersonal skills from corporate leaders.

Engaging or replacing complacent distributors to ensure growth

Companies are also stepping up their efforts by pressuring distributors to improve performance and proactively contribute to growth. One of my clients says:

"I noticed that many of our distributors in CEEMEA had started to take their contract with us for granted. Some have become fantastically rich: they worked little, raced their cars, sailed around the world or travelled for fun. They became complacent. So when I challenged them to talk about faster growth, it sometimes looked like we are talking two different languages. The question then becomes obvious. Do we try and bring them on board, or do we go through the hassle of replacing our distributor with also questionable results? Over the last 12 months, I managed to replace three of our distributors with younger, hungrier organizations. Two out of three are now working in line with our ambitious targets."

In addition to replacing distributors, companies are also setting up strict sales targets and frequent reporting structures, as well as contracts with shorter horizons (and which include about a million clauses as to why a multinational could discontinue the contract). Another client in the healthcare industry who is running CEEMEA markets told me:

"We decided we wanted to accelerate growth in the region over the next five years and recognized that we were not satisfied with many of our distributors there. After several unhappy experiences playing hardball with them, we shifted to a philosophy of engagement. Our staff have now come up with a number of initiatives that through a combination of incentives and motivations puts the distributor on our growth path."

Sometimes neither engagement nor hard ball helps. I find this to be a frequent issue in some Middle Eastern jurisdictions. One of the MEA presidents for an industrial firm said:

"Our relationship with two of our critical distributors in Saudi Arabia and Kuwait got so complicated that we could not engage them and we feared getting out of the contract, since they threatened legal action if we discontinued the contracts. So we made an agreement with them that they would still get their agency/distributor fees but asked them not do any work for us, except physical distribution. We took charge of our growth plan and it is working well."

Companies should also make sure they provide enough and regular training for distributors. This helps distributors feel like part of the corporate family and, most importantly, ensures that distributors are always familiar with products but are also trained to follow marketing and sales initiatives, to understand the financial boundaries, etc.

Helping your distributor (and even customers) financially

In difficult economic times, companies are increasingly helping their distributors financially, usually by acting as a bank or taking their distributors to the bank the multinational uses. In many emerging markets, working capital is either hard to come by or still quite expensive for small- and medium-sized firms, and corporate assistance is all about ensuring that growth plans are not interrupted because of distributors' financial weakness.

Of course, ideally you do not want to be with a distributor who suffers financial difficulties, but in the aftermath of the global crisis there are liquidity problems emerging, even within otherwise solid distributors. Perhaps they work in a country where interest rates rose unexpectedly and their debt burden is squeezing liquidity, or they are not getting paid on time by retailers. Whatever the reason, companies should retain a flexible attitude and step in with funds if need be.

Here are several examples of companies increasingly acting as banks. One of my clients in the health care equipment sector reported:

> "Ever since we started with extensive leasing arrangements run through our internal leasing house, our sales have been booming, even in markets that we otherwise considered as too depressed."

Another executive in the IT industry said:

> "We have our internal finance arm that caters to B2B customers all over the world, and without this we would not be growing as fast as we are growing now. It took us a long time to set up but it is a fantastic service."

In the consumer goods industry, one of the large multinationals reported:

> "We are increasingly extending long finance terms to those distributors who for some reason can't order in line with our wishes. The headquarters now understand that we must trust our partners more. Ever since we started extending payment terms to what was previously considered too long, we only had a problem in two countries out of 115, with a distributor taking advantage or disappearing with our receivables. Extending financing is important to maintain our growth momentum. We can't afford to lose it."

Another company in the cosmetics industry reports:

> "We are probably one of the largest micro finance houses in world. We extend loans worth from tens of dollars to several hundred dollars to our buyers. After some initial nervousness we now realize our non-performing loan portfolio is actually lower than in almost any bank we benchmarked with. Without this arrangement, our emerging market business would not even be half the size of the current one."

Distributor competition

Corporate opinion is largely divided into two camps when it comes to giving exclusivity to distributors. Some are dead against it, while some think it is a good idea for distributors to have a chance to compete against each other in well-defined geographic areas – then natural selection decides who is the best to run the operation. In smaller markets companies are increasingly opting for exclusive distributors but with shorter-term contracts (and with many opt-out clauses included). In some of the large markets, such as the BRIC countries (Brazil, Russia, India and China), countries are so big that it is often hard to find distributors with nationwide coverage that are able satisfy increasingly ambitious corporate growth targets.

Compliance monitoring

Companies are also increasing their compliance monitoring of distributors. Global and country level compliance regulations are getting tighter, with significantly more severe punishments for those who break the rules. Up until about 1997, many European companies could even treat bribes paid for international contracts as a tax-deductible expense. Those days are behind us and today most developed market legislation make both companies and individuals liable in cases of bribery.

The big change in recent years is that even if distributors pay bribes to win business, corporate executives in multinational companies responsible for those territories could end up in jail. For that reason, companies are working hard to leave a very clear paper trail that demonstrates that the company has informed its distributors that bribes will not be accepted to win business. Companies are also monitoring the activities of their distributors much more closely and report internally any suspicious transactions or business that was gained under suspicious circumstances.

LIMIT THE POTENTIAL FOR YOUR LEADERS TO PRIVATELY BENEFIT BY DOUBLE-CHECKING WHO THEY HIRE AS DISTRIBUTORS

Two recent examples of this type of corruption are symptomatic of an increasing trend within multinationals. One executive from a consumer goods industry reported:

> "We were wondering why our former regional president was stopping by the office so frequently after he retired. At first we thought it was because he could not really switch off, because he cared about the business he had built over the years – we felt sorry he did not have hobbies to keep him busy. But then we realized he was actually closely monitoring if we were still working with a number of major distributors in our territory. We became suspicious and after a long investigation, we found out that he was the co-owner of several distributor companies – in fact he co-founded them and then channeled millions of business to himself when he was running things. And he wanted to make sure this arrangement continued."

Another regional director of an industrial firm discovered that three of his country managers were getting kick-backs from distributors. "The message from our country directors to distributors was simple: I will renew your contract if you pay me [x] amount each year. This had been happening for a long time and explained why one of our former country directors was able to afford a Ferrari!"

ASSESS IF IT MAKES SENSE TO BUY OUT LOCAL DISTRIBUTORS

In high growth markets many companies have come to the conclusion that the only way to grow quickly is to actually take over the distributor organization and significantly increase control over the business. Various examples that I have come across show that more control over business usually means more sustainable growth over the medium and long term and outperforming the competition. Purchases of distributors tend to be motivated by a number of factors including:

- A distributor who is unwilling or unable to follow the new growth strategy
- A distributor wanting, or being forced, to sell
- The threat of a distributor migrating to the competition because of better deals.

This is not a strategy that companies should embrace for all markets, but for strategic markets, in terms of growth potential it is a good approach that few companies have regretted. While it is sometimes difficult to convince headquarters of such an expense, a number of good examples show that business tends to improve with more direct control. This "control over business" is also seen as a key success factor for the future as competitive pressures increase beyond recognition.

BE FLEXIBLE IN APPROACHING DISTRIBUTION CHALLENGES

Achieving nationwide distribution that consistently supports growth objectives in emerging markets is not an easy task. This is where operational ability either excels or prevents companies from reaching their objectives. Distribution networks are often inefficient and extremely fragmented. In some markets, such as in Sub-Saharan Africa for example, the task of distributing the product borders on almost impossible.

This is why companies are changing their approach and embracing the fact that in a number of markets the approach has to be flexible. One executive from the IT industry illustrates an approach that is consistent with the majority of firms' views today.

> "The markets are so complicated that one approach is simply not covering all sales opportunities. So we are using multiple channels. We handle a number of large key accounts directly. Many are covered through local partners and IT integrators and we co-ordinate them closely with our local staff. In some geographically large markets, such as Russia and India, we even have agents that just sell on commission. They work in territories where our local distributors and partners are not present. And we have local teams co-ordinating these agents, monitoring when some of them might 'grow up' to become a full partner or distributor. The philosophy for the future is simple: we will do whatever works or whatever the market requires. That is a big change for our large company and it works very well."

FOCUS ON CLOSING ANY GEOGRAPHIC AND CUSTOMER/CONSUMER GAPS

Once they have carried out a proper analysis of the geographies in which they operate and the extent of their existing customer base, many multinationals can find gaps. Often, they find that they are not equally represented in all provinces or secondary/tertiary cities. Many also realize that they under-penetrate rural areas. And when one maps the full range of potential customers in a country, there are inevitably large gaps for the vast majority of firms.

The strategic goal for the near future for companies that I work with is to focus on closing such gaps. Part of the gap will be filled directly by the multinationals, but local distributors and partners also have to step in, too. A number of B2B firms that I work with have recently created what one of my clients called a "war room for emerging markets". He went on to explain:

> "We put large pieces of paper on the wall of our largest meeting rooms in all countries and we wrote down the entire 'universe' of customers that our research had identified. There were so many gaps. We circled them in red. Once these areas became ours we painted them in green. The strategic goal in every country in which we operate is to turn the walls into a green colour. Luckily, global HQ is behind the project and has decided to finance on the ground expansion, too. But without some local depth of involvement, our walls will remain largely red."

PRICING
ASSESS YOUR ABILITY TO GROW THROUGH PRICING

Interestingly, most companies that I work with generate more profit than revenues from emerging markets as a percentage of their total global profit or as a percentage of total global sales. For example, if the Middle East North Africa region accounts for, on average, 3% of global sales, the same area can generate 4% of global profits (in some firms even more). But this will change for at least two reasons. First, companies will need to reinvest more of their profits back into the business, increasing spending on building a local presence and brand-building. Second, rising competition will slowly chip away at sometimes very attractive margins.

Still, many of my clients have been pleasantly surprised that in a number of emerging markets price sensitivity is sometimes lower than in the developed world. But pricing potential needs to be looked at in a granular way. I am not talking here about across-the-board increases in prices. This needs to be smart: targeted in order to avoid a backlash from buyers and to avoid losing hard-earned market positions. But experiments in this pricing area have often resulted in surprisingly positive outcomes.

> "Do not quote me on this, but our strategy for a number of emerging markets is to keep prices very high. We realize that in several of our premium segments, customers buy more whenever we increase the price. It is a matter of prestige for many locals and now part of our emerging markets growth is through

sometimes savage price increases," says a director of a major consumer goods firm.

BE CAREFUL WITH PRICING WHEN TIMES ARE TOUGH – PRESERVE YOUR MARKET SHARE

I often come across firms that increased market share by allowing longer payment terms when times were tough or when currencies in emerging markets temporarily fell against major currencies. As one regional director said:

> "We have decided that it is much more important to keep and increase share than alienate our distributors and customers with shorter payment terms, prepayment or price increases designed to move short-term margins up."

Some companies cannot do this as global headquarters insist that profits denominated in dollars, euros or yen stay the same. This leaves little choice for country or regional managers but to raise prices (to earn the same amount in dollars or euros). One senior executive from an agro-food industry reported:

> "When currencies in many emerging markets fell during September 2011, we quickly told our guys on the ground to raise prices. Today, we can see this was a mistake. We lost a number of customers in the last two months in Latin America, Central Europe and in parts of Africa. We have now reversed the decision and told our managers on the ground to go back to

pricing that is acceptable to our customers. We know the currencies will bounce back and now we think we can take a short term hit on profits denominated in dollars. All of this is very difficult to explain to headquarters."

IF YOU ARE IN MARKETS WITH LESS COMPETITION, USE HIGHER PRICES TO BOOST MARGINS – AT LEAST UNTIL THE COMPETITION ARRIVES

Markets with little competition are now few and far between. Even in Sub-Saharan Africa, margins are slowly getting tighter as more companies arrive. But when companies carry out their competitive mapping on a regular basis (see Chapter 2), it should be possible to keep prices higher in certain segments, usually for a limited amount of time. So try to get some short-term profitability growth through pricing. I frequently interact with executives active in Africa and many use this approach since there is still very limited competition in a number of sectors.

CONTROL PRICING IN THE CHANNEL

Only through close, on-the-ground presence and co-ordination with partners and distributors can companies make sure their distributors, resellers or retailers are not playing with pricing. The last thing you want is for your price to be too high for the final buyers and lose share because of it. Also, you do not want prices too low either in order to preserve brand perception in the market.

ADJUST TO LOCAL PRICE POINTS

I have looked at this aspect already in rethinking innovation (see beginning of this chapter), but it is worth repeating the mantra. It is important to have products across a variety of market segments in the future. Regions and countries are not uniform. Even in the poorest markets companies find multiple market segments at different price points. To achieve medium- to long-term growth, most companies will eventually compete in multiple segments – it is just a question of time.

Some additional B2B marketing wisdom

Executives that sell business-to-business continue to have a number of key challenges in the fast-moving emerging markets. They include: generating high quality leads, managing volatile, unpredictable and sometimes long sales cycles and maximizing value of each lead, customer retention and loyalty.

A corporate consensus is emerging that despite all the advances in social media, etc, no one should forget how much face-to-face relationships with key users, key potentials and key hot leads truly matter. Firms must maintain face-to-face contact in order to ensure marketing execution and ability to close deals. The question many firms are now asking is: do they have enough staff talking to all decisions makers and those key influencers? The idea is to nurture the relationships with all influencers during good times and bad.

As B2B relationships evolve in emerging markets, there is a noticeable shift of emphasis to more measurable channels and less mass marketing. I notice, generally speaking, that there is an increase in spending on social media, targeted events for clients, search engine optimization, white papers, website design and PR, and that there is a steady decrease in direct mail, print ads and trade shows. Firms are increasingly asking if marketing messages and sales collateral are in line with needs in each country and segment of the market in terms of price, sector and customer. They ask how the message is different for those who are really looking for solutions compared to those who are just "sort of" interested? A number of firms are shifting marketing operations to a country, and even customer level, strategy. Strategies are emphasizing the measurable. How can your product improve a customer's company, save money and grow revenues? Many firms that I work with now integrate sales and marketing into a joint revenue pipeline and co-ordinate the two more closely. Many executives told me that they are adamant that prospectors must start the buying process long before they speak to sales so the alignment of that sequence leads to deals.

Other activities that B2B marketers are doing include elevated emphasis on excellence in service, proactively going after competitors' business, and building war rooms in each office to close customer and geographic gaps.

There is a growing emphasis on nurturing leads and making sure this capability in each country is second to none. Each lead in an emerging market presents a shrinking window of opportunity. Competitors are fast and companies must make sure they embrace each lead with full speed and competence.

"We let our distributors run our marketing and after several years of doing reasonably well, we noticed we started to lose share. Once we took control, our fortunes changed beyond recognition. In my office, you can see a poster with the slogan: 'Do not let distributors and partners run marketing'. It is a reminder for everyone who ever comes into my office that we should never, ever go that route again," says a senior regional executive of a large chemical company.

Marketing and selling to governments

Companies dependent on public sector business are using many aspects of the B2B wisdom described above. Many are perfectly applicable. But in addition, I see that companies usually hope for large public sector business without necessarily investing in enough corporate affairs or external affairs staff. I am deeply convinced that the only way to increase share in the public sector business is to nurture personal relationships at different government levels, and to keep doing this. It is crucial to continually develop goodwill among officials. And this is not only about perhaps supporting their pet projects with donations or making them look good in the eyes of colleagues or the public. It really is about developing genuine personal relationships at the local level. This is why many firms that are dependent on public sector business are investing heavily in having enough staff on the ground to develop these relationships.

Some markets, such as those in the Middle East, China or Russia, are notoriously difficult to develop relationships with government officials and require more staff on the ground for that purpose. And yet, too many firms either do not have anyone in corporate affairs, or they have three or four corporate ambassadors based in regional or global headquarters, who spend most of their time flying between various countries for just a few days at a time. This used to be enough: today, relationships need to be developed at a local level. It also makes sense to use various diplomatic channels to open doors with various government offices.

CHAPTER 4

HUMAN RESOURCES WISDOM FOR THE FUTURE[2]

Press on. Nothing in the world can take the place of persistence. Talent will not; there is nothing more common than unsuccessful men with talent. Genius will not; unrewarded genius is almost a proverb. Education will not; the world is full of educated derelicts. Persistence and determination alone are omnipotent."

—*Calvin Coolidge*

ALL EXECUTIVES AGREE that getting the human resources equation right in emerging markets is an incredibly important foundation for sustainable growth and to outperform competition. Winning the war for talent in emerging markets is a strategic imperative. Most companies now realize that their labour pool is migrating from being an enabler of growth (through availability of abundant, cheap labour) to a driver of growth (as labour-force skills and know-how develop). In the end, companies can only outperform the competition and grow in a sustainable way in emerging markets if they find and retain great people.

But the number of challenges involved in getting this right for the future is enormous. Competition for talent is genuinely increasing

---

[2] This chapter was written in co-operation with Sanja Haas (strategic/retention HR issues) and Antonija Pacek (building creativity in organizations). See page 271 for their short biographies.

in virtually all emerging markets and just like competitive products, it is coming from unexpected corners. Emerging market multinationals poach good staff and overpay them. Purely local firms do the same. Great managers are neither cheap, nor abundant in most emerging markets. Supply is low and demand getting permanently hotter in almost all emerging geographies (except those CEE markets affected by the deleveraging that I describe in the last chapter, or a few markets in the Arab world affected by the disruption of the "Arab Spring"). No company can afford to lose the battle for talent in emerging markets today.

Corporations today are struggling with numerous HR-related challenges in emerging markets. It is time to holistically and globally re-think current HR practices and employee value mindsets. This will allow companies to manage their challenges, stand out against key competition and enable them to outperform, on a global scale, all those companies that are not at the forefront of innovative, revised, breakthrough and fully integrated HR approaches. These include:
- creative recruitment
- breakthrough retention strategies
- strong focus on learning and development with an ROI mindset
- putting creativity and innovation at the top of the individual and organizational development agenda

This chapter will examine each of these in turn, exploring why it is important to address all in a holistic, integrated manner and how they relate to white collar HR issues in emerging markets.

TRENDS IN RECRUITMENT
BE CREATIVE WHEN HIRING AND MAKING OFFERS

As competition for talent heats up, you have to outperform your competition in the search for the right people. Companies are now using multiple channels to find the best and the brightest, and then offering them deals that are hard to refuse (more on how to retain your staff later). In addition to the usual searches by big global headhunting names or advertising, companies are increasingly using a combination of well-established, regional or purely local headhunters, who know people who are very familiar with local markets and have a track record in those markets. A growing number of firms find that they have to extend a search globally if they want to find experienced senior leaders. I see firms looking for Arab speakers in Australia, asking them if they would want to come and work in Dubai. I see emigré Russians living in Canada being asked to go back home. I see Brazilians in the US being asked to return to Brazil. The search for the best is now a local, regional and global exercise – all in one.

Internal HR departments are increasingly tracking key managers in competitors' firms, assessing their performance from a distance. The idea is to identify a few top individuals who could be brought in at some stage and if needed. Companies find this to be a more reliable thing than reading someone's CV once the search begins. Companies also increasingly over-hire to avoid gaps that can puncture a growth momentum. And companies are increasingly waiting for the right person rather than going for someone too quickly who does not feel right.

SEEK ENTREPRENEURS AND "MASTERS OF BUSINESS CREATION"

What kind of criteria is being used to make sure you get the right people who can deliver your future growth? Things are shifting on this front, too. As companies increasingly move responsibility to local offices, they realize that country level leaders, for example, must also be entrepreneurial individuals. "We want these guys to sort of own these businesses, because we are decentralizing quite a few of our functions and giving locals more authority, responsibility and freedom to operate," says one global HR director of a major consumer electronics firms.

Companies that want to increase their local presence are now devising ways to test and measure a candidate's entrepreneurial skills. At the same time, companies should not be under the illusion they will actually hire genuine entrepreneurs. The real ones are out there, running their own businesses and making millions – and they hate to take orders. They will not want to settle for corporate life under any circumstances. On the other hand, companies are now extraordinarily careful about not ending up with what one of my Austrian clients calls "Corporate *Beamten*", which loosely translates as, "people who work in for-profit corporations but behave like public servants or non-profit guys".

Look at the track record of candidates and how they delivered growth consistently over time. Examine whether they are just good cost cutters, or they actually have a track record of growing the top line. Make sure they are not the type of guys who maximize profits for two or three years and then move on to another role or country. Probe in great depth how top line growth was achieved. Look for those who have passed truly high-end leadership training so that they know how to work with people. Look for what I call MBCs – "Masters of Business Creation" – rather than MBAs. (By the way: it is about time business schools started to produce MBCs in addition to MBAs.)

The attitude of candidates matters more than ever. Those with experience must demonstrate a "can do" attitude. Senior executives also note that those familiar with a geographic area/country and sector tend to do better than those who are not familiar. Local language skill is crucial for country leadership positions.

BUILD LOCAL TALENT

Expats are a dying breed, unless they get entrenched in a local culture, learn the language and want to live on the ground for a long time. Short-term, three-year expat assignments for country directors are something that companies are increasingly trying to avoid, for at least two reasons.

First, short-term assignments tend to create incentives for country leaders to extract a lot of profit growth from markets so they can advance their own career. Often, sadly, this is done at the expense of nurturing long-term business. "Almost any fool can boost profits in the short-term, but what are the medium- and long-term consequences of such actions?" asks one regional executive.

Second, sometimes, just as a manager has gotten familiar with a market or language, he has moved on to another location.

This approach is simply not effective in building consistent and sustainable results in tricky growth markets. Remember that the key is to nurture relationships. By the time key customers, government officials and staff become familiar with a country leader, he leaves. The company loses so much needed continuity.

At the same time, expat staff retain some advantages. This is especially true in larger strategic markets, which are supposed to be the engines of growth in absolute and percentage terms in the future. CEOs like to appoint trusted, long-standing employees to such strategic positions, and this is understandable. But companies are now trying to extend the tenure of such expats, so they stay in certain countries and geographies for at least five to six years, and ideally much longer. And such expats are tasked with mentoring their local replacements.

BRING IN INTERNAL STAFF FROM DEVELOPED MARKETS

Companies are also increasingly sourcing for the best employees in their own offices in the developed world. As developed world businesses struggle and growth happens elsewhere, many firms have proactively sought to relocate people who are hungry for action and growth to emerging geographies. Some firms have had to reduce the size of their operations in the developed world in the last few years but at the same time did not want to lose people in whom they had invested so much. And many were happy to relocate when offered such opportunities. Some of the managers in the developed world are simply bored with stagnant markets and a "protect what we have" mindset. Many would prefer to live and work in faster-paced environments and companies are trying to identify those less motivated ones and offer them opportunities in higher growth markets that are "less boring".

A MORE PROACTIVE APPROACH IS NEEDED WITH THE YOUNG ONES

Some firms insist they only promote from within and therefore continue to put enormous emphasis on getting the right people as they graduate or, ideally, even before they graduate. But even for those who hire both inexperienced and experienced staff, the process of vetting those young ones is also moving at a different speed and becoming more creative.

The goal, needless to say, is to pick the crème de la crème before they actually move into the job market. A number of companies are beefing up their links with universities to try and identify the best and brightest early in the game. They offer scholarships, bring those students to their firms to work during the summers for attractive pay, get them involved with projects to gain some fresh blood and ideas. Job offers often follow for some of the best before they actually graduate. In the relentless war for talent amid emerging market talent shortages, it is important to have a pool of young, bright people from which to source.

USE TOUGH ECONOMIC TIMES TO PICK THE BEST

When economic times are tough, companies should be on the lookout for those people that have been laid off by corporations that have closed some offices and discarded some superb individuals just to protect a quarterly budget report (and the budget holder's ass). Such individuals can be found in the developed world at the moment or in some low-growth, depressed markets in Central Eastern Europe. "Some real jewels are out there at the moment. We are focusing on finding people with skills sets and experiences we do not necessarily have in-house, such as running businesses at lower price points, for example. Or who have long experience in really difficult or smaller markets," said one regional director in the IT industry.

HIRE EVEN WHEN YOU DON'T NEED ANYONE

I have noticed over the last few years that many long-term oriented firms that want consistent growth in emerging markets hire even when they do not need anyone. Despite new and well-designed retention strategies (see the next point on retention practices), seasoned executives still note that turnover in hot emerging markets continue to exceed that of the developed world. This is not surprising, considering the tremendous demand and often inadequate supply of top-notch individuals.

So many firms are continually looking for newcomers to join their organization, sometimes just to take part in a bunch of training programs and a few special projects.

> "We figure by the time an individual gains some experience with us, someone else will have left. So instead of wasting time finding a replacement, we are simply nurturing a pool of talented, trained individuals who are already familiar with our company and our products," says an HR director of a major multinational.

The ultimate goal of this exercise is to ensure certain growth initiatives do not fall into a vacuum until a replacement is found. Another executive says:

> "There is so much competition that we can ill-afford to lose any time. The last thing I want is to miss a quarterly budget because for a few months I did not have anyone to do the work. If I miss the quarterly budget it means I might be asked to start cutting costs and still deliver on top line growth with reduced resources. That is a headache I do not need and that is why we have a deliberate policy to over-hire. I find this to be a tremendous competitive advantage and key for consistent growth delivery."

RETENTION STRATEGIES
RETENTION OF THE BEST PEOPLE IS THE KEY TO SUCCESS – BREAK AND CHANGE CORPORATE RULES IF NEED BE AND EXECUTE METICULOUSLY

Retention is one HR challenge that dominates all the "people" discussions I have ever had with senior executives in so many emerging markets. And things are getting worse: although the pool of well-trained managers is increasing, the increase is often simply not matching ever-increasing demand. Multinationals are getting more aggressive in emerging markets and hiring more people, but this is also the case for local and emerging market multinationals. And prices for people (especially the best managers and leaders) are going up and will continue to go up in many faster growth markets.

To design a good retention strategy, companies must first understand both the retention equation in each emerging market and the key drivers for retaining people in certain geographies. One executive sums up overheated markets well:

> "My managers in certain countries are getting better offers all the time. Most of our competitors have either increased presence or are planning to do so. The easiest way to start up a local office is to hire people like our staff, whom we trained over the years and who know the industry, contacts and players inside out. The competition is looking for growth quickly and they do not have time to send an expat who will need a year or two to get things moving. And they do not want some novice from another industry for the same reason. They come in and offer really good deals to our managers that they find difficult to refuse."

So what should companies do to improve their retention? My advice to companies is to first change their internal mindset. Forget the rules you have that apply in America or Western Europe or Japan. Accept that your finance director in Moscow, Sao Paolo or Istanbul might be more expensive than the one in Stockholm, Houston or Osaka. Accept that you have to pay in line with local supply and demand, rather than some globally imposed pay scales. Accept that the price differential could even increase in the next few years.

The same applies to pay increases. So many firms still use a global guideline when it comes to annual salary increases, such as not paying anyone more than 3%. Others say to their regional guys: "You can increase your overall salary cost for existing staff by 2.83% – but you decide who gets a bit more and who gets less." But that is utterly unhelpful and detrimental to retention when it comes to so many emerging markets, where annual salaries can go up between 5% and 20% (or even more if the inflation rate is quite high) per year on average.

The main point to understand is this: if you want to keep the best people, you have to pay in line with local supply and demand, and you have to deliver pay increases in the same way. This is the bedrock of good staff retention. There are other factors of course, but if you get this one wrong, you can pursue other policies as much as you want and you will still lose a proportion of your best people.

That HR costs are becoming overheated in emerging markets is illustrated by the following short anecdote from one of my long-standing clients.

> "Within the same week, two of my country managers came to me with the same message. They were approached by local conglomerates, who offered to double their pay if they would move to them. Both are fantastic over-achievers and worryingly they were running two large strategic markets – Russia and South Africa. They were long-standing employees on whom we wanted to rely to drive our growth in CIS and Sub-Saharan Africa in the future. They

were too important to lose. Both said they would accept the offers unless we matched them. I could understand that it was simply too tempting for them. I told them that the corporation would be unlikely to agree, but I promised I would try to give them salaries that are higher than my own. When I argued their case a few weeks later in the US, I was positively surprised when our new CEO (who was for a long time active in Asia and Eastern Europe and understood what I was talking about) agreed to give them 85% of what they wanted in base pay, plus a tremendous long-term incentive if they stayed with us for five years, and even more if they stayed for ten. I am happy to say that both stayed on. We are now doing this regularly for our best staff. With these two guys, we are fully on track to overachieve on growth targets."

This little story illustrates that companies who break the corporate rules on pay and (especially medium to long-term) incentives can reap great growth and earnings benefits for a relatively low cost. In both of these cases, the investment was just over half a million dollars in initial cash outlay and the sales upside they delivered was literally measured in over $100 million per year. As a company that wants more sustainable success in emerging markets, you do not want to jeopardize your growth plan for a few hundred thousand dollars. You would spend the same amount trying to find a replacement anyway.

REMEMBER THAT REPLACEMENT COSTS ARE HIGH – GET RETENTION STRATEGIES RIGHT

The direct costs of replacing an employee include advertising, headhunter fees and sign-on bonuses. These can run to the equivalent of six months salary for an hourly employee to 150–250% for a sales or managerial position. Importantly, the direct replacement costs are only the tip of the iceberg. There are also indirect costs, such as service disruption, loss of corporate knowledge and a knock-on effect of lower morale and motivation in the group surrounding the departing employee. This type of disruption is actually more severe in emerging markets than in the developed world due to the preponderance of relationship-based types of business. While difficult to quantify, these effects are real and take a toll on the company's results.

With this savings opportunity in mind, a company can justify funding a retention and development strategy, which will not only keep precious talent in the company, but also highly motivated and working at its peak. Some of this money can also be reinvested into further developing corporate talent, thereby advancing the company's ability to deliver breakthrough results.

Companies must benchmark pay levels in each country where they have staff or where they planted a person in a distributors' offices. This is increasingly done at least twice a year, since in some markets pay levels can jump quickly – sometimes purely because of an overheated demand, at other times because of a higher inflation rate (and sometimes both).

EMPLOYEE NEEDS

What is the objective of a retention strategy? A retention strategy must be designed to engender employee loyalty. Particularly in developing markets, companies often believe that employees leave simply because the financial incentives are higher elsewhere – that the employees are "bought". And of course, this is often correct. If companies don't want to get into a salary war, there is little chance of retaining an employee.

In many cases, however, the higher salary at the new company sometimes only appeals to the employee who is "open" to other offers – that is, the employee who feels somewhat disconnected from the company mission, values or leadership, or who is unhappy in their relationship with the management (the latter is really important in many emerging markets). In order to retain the employee, this relationship building must be done proactively and consistently so that the employee is not interested in hearing propositions from other employers.

A simple framework can be used to explain the way loyalty building fits into an "employee hierarchy of needs".

At the bottom level of the pyramid are compensation and base benefits. This level of connection with the employee is related to the employee's ability to "pay the bills". This compensation aspect must be correct in absolute terms for the employee to want to stay with the company.

At the second level is a traditional set of benefits. "Traditional" varies by market, but could include things such as insurance, cars, meals and other elements. Like salary, these must also meet at least a basic level in order for the employee to remain satisfied with the company. However, because these kinds of benefits are frequently determined and benchmarked by wider practice, they become commoditized and over time revert to hygiene factors, rather than something special that differentiates the relationship between the company and the employee.

At the third level are personalized benefits and programs. This set of initiatives distinguishes a company from its peers and allow the employee to personalize the value proposition. The ability to personalize also means that the benefit package can evolve to fit changing employee needs, thereby deepening the engagement and motivation on an ongoing basis.

The top level of the pyramid is a set of behaviours that define personal relationships within the company. These are truly personal and culturally sensitive. They include things as large or as small as the way the manager interacts with the employee. For example, in China it would be important for a manager to inquire about an employee's family and to seriously consider concessions and special benefits linked to family circumstances. The critical element of this part of the pyramid is to get to know the employee and interact with them in a way that charms him or her. A happy employee not only results in a lower turnover of staff, but will also drive higher motivation. The lack of turnover and higher motivation will lead to a higher level of productivity and therefore better corporate results.

PROVIDING BENEFITS, DRIVING MOTIVATION AND PRODUCTIVITY

The question then arises as to how to design an Employee Value Proposition (EVP) that delivers great results in building employee engagement and drives the company toward its objectives? When executed correctly, creating a set of benefits that the employee values greatly not only increases loyalty to the company, but it also increases employee satisfaction and motivation, which leads to higher productivity. Companies have to identify a set of benefits that can simultaneously increase loyalty to the company and enhance performance on the job.

Employers can differentiate themselves from the competition by way of financial and non-financial benefits. These benefits necessarily need to vary by location, since what is important in one location is not necessarily as valuable elsewhere. A program to assist employees in securing a mortgage can be a huge motivator. For employees in countries where mortgages are readily available and housing relatively cheaper, this may be seen as less of a game-changing benefit. In some markets companies provide stock options even for relatively low-level employees. Or they provide scholarships for their children, or extend corporate loans to key employees for other purchases. In some locations, cars are given to very young employees because this is what the local market expects.

The benefits and programs also need to be flexible and the employee should, ideally, be able to choose from a "menu" of items in order to tailor to personal needs that evolve over time. For example, flexibility in working hours may be important when an employee is faced with child- or elder-care issues, but it may be less important during other phases in their life. Or it may be more relevant only in certain countries: for example sabbaticals, flexiwork and teleworking is becoming increasingly attractive in India, whereas the training of leadership skills is seen as a key benefit in China. Also, recently there seems to be a growing trend among young Chinese employees to take *Luoci* ("naked resignation") – i.e., these young professionals leave work just to "rest" as they are "exhausted". Hence a thought-through, work–life balance corporate benefit is increasingly attractive and has the potential to become a key competitive advantage in the near future.

The easiest way to clarify the value of different benefits is to ask employees either directly or by establishing pilot programs. You will soon establish if a "concierge" service or gourmet food benefits are more appreciated by the employees. Creativity is paramount, as is the recognition that it is not always the company that needs to fund the programs. Sometimes the employees are happy to pay for services made available to them and have a high appreciation level of simply having services "at their fingertips". Sensitivity and experimentation will provide the most accurate level of understanding as to which benefits best drive motivation and productivity.

It is also important to keep the menu of benefit options flexible and changing. Some benefits and programs may be extremely successful at certain times, with their relative importance fading later. Designing a package of benefits, therefore, is not a one-off exercise, but an on-going part of HR work.

Programs in this area need not be only financial in nature. Involving an individual in their career planning and development can be an important motivator. People want to see that there is a development plan for them – including career advancement. Ensuring employees have sufficient knowledge and understanding about the system and process *and* how this links to their personal growth is key.

RETENTION STRATEGIES AND PERSONALIZATION

Re-framing the cost of turnover and the benefit of retention will enable a company to choose to invest in a retention strategy. Re-thinking the company's relationship with the employee through a retention lens will then lead to a set of practices designed to personalize the employee experience. The result is an enhanced ability to attract and retain a workforce that is motivated and productive. These practices can help the company succeed in emerging markets. However, in order to maximize success, they must be combined with the retention "partner concept" – a tailored development strategy that focuses on the needs of both the company and employees.

"Personalization" is the key unifying concept in a successful retention and development strategy. The workforce can no longer be viewed as a single unit or a commodity – they must be seen and treated as individuals, with unique needs and wishes. Designing corporate strategies which are on the one hand scalable and on the other hand tailored will be the sweet spot companies have to reach to succeed in the war for talent.

While each of these concepts is crucial in developing markets, they can also easily be applied to any market. As "Generation Y" has a bigger and bigger presence in the workforce, the concept of personalization of the employee experience will be crucial for companies to set themselves apart. Thus, designing a workforce strategy for developing countries can provide a learning opportunity for the entire company and thus a winning strategy on a global scale.

MAKE SURE YOU KNOW YOUR EMPLOYEES REALLY WELL

A regional director of one of the largest chemical firms in the world told me:

> "We have this internal mantra about knowing our customers, but we only got to know our employees in offices in emerging markets during exit interviews. We now systematically interview our staff in emerging markets while they are still employed to make sure we keep track of their happiness, motivation and needs. Ever since we started this three years ago, retention has improved, partly because it made us realize we were underpaying in some markets. We also discovered who the bad country level leaders were and we replaced them."

EMPLOY AN ASSET MANAGEMENT MINDSET

Place both strategic efforts and money behind statements such as "people are our key asset", or as Reichheld & Teal stated: "We need to see people as assets. Asset defection is unacceptable. Human capital, unlike other assets, does not depreciate over time. It actually improves with age."

And assets need to be developed. On average, companies today spend approximately 5% of their turnover on R&D. Alone, the top global pharmaceutical, biotechnological, technical equipment and automobile companies spent US $200 billion in R&D in 2010. This compares to an annual total investment of US $70 billion for executive education among global companies. Hence, from a purely quantitative approach, this falls below the classic R&D investment, and marginalizes the strategic intent of investing in, and developing, the key corporate asset, i.e., people. Therefore, changing this mindset is the first crucial step.

Secondly, earmarking and transparently communicating a certain percentage of the annual turnover for people development will send the right signals to employees and key stakeholders about the company's intent to elevate investment in people (and therefore "oiling" the organization for future growth) to a scale which, at a minimum, matches the R&D investments in products, services or technology. Finally, being very clear on the strategic benefits and specific objectives of development is crucial.

Why have a development strategy at all? On a strategic level, if talent is a strategic imperative, the need to develop talent becomes a priority in and of itself. On a pragmatic, operational level, merely retaining and motivating employees will not deliver the bottom line – corporations need to be at the forefront of business/industry developments by "upgrading" the skill set of their workforce, especially in highly dynamic emerging markets. Also, since companies sometimes find that local education systems are not delivering people with the right kinds of skills, there arises a need to either achieve the impossible or deciding to recruit for potential with the intention (and the funds!) to then develop these recruits internally.

DEVELOPMENT STRATEGY OBJECTIVES

What is the objective of a development strategy? A development strategy must be designed to ensure individuals have the right skills, at the right time, in the right place and at the right cost. Hence it must be very carefully planned both in terms of needs, delivery and desired results, for both present and future business and individual needs. It can also serve as a great retention objective – for example, research shows that the number one most valued employee benefit for the (knowledge hungry) Generation Y is training and development.

The corporate development plan can be designed around a very simplistic framework based on three steps:
- analyzing needs
- deciding what, how and where to develop
- development reward and recognition

We will examine these points in turn.

Analyzing needs

This process begins with having a mindset that accepts it is OK to recruit for potential versus skills because a well-oiled corporate development system will ensure the new employees are up and running in minimal time. This approach would help ease the pressure on a lot of the recruiting efforts in India, Brazil and the Middle East, for example, where workforce readiness is low.

Next, corporations need to take a hard, critical look at which technical, functional and leadership/people skills are key to developing overall, and which are specific to different individuals and business units – both for the present but also five years into the future.

The final step involves understanding internal capabilities – is it possible to develop internally from a global (and not merely local) perspective? For example, do we have the right set-up/capabilities on a global scale, or do we need to use external suppliers? The latter will prove to be difficult in most emerging countries due to the quality and choice of local vendors being limited. However, keeping the asset management mindset, looking at this from a global perspective could prove dramatically different, as opposed to being focused on what the local country can provide.

Deciding what, how and where to develop

Leadership and people skills are very much linked to the global corporate culture ("how things gets done around here and according to what principles"), while functional and technical skills are driven by the job content/need. Some skills are better developed on the job, others in formal classroom settings. In addition, development needs to be tailored to country specificities (for example, which labour regulations need to be considered when training employees in Brazil); to employee-specific needs or interests (for example, Generation Y might find the use of gaming as a development tool incredibly appealing); and to take into account cultural considerations.

For example, key leadership skills can be taught that will help employees work on a community project, such as how to develop rural Chinese villages into commercial and competitive units (a topic very close to the Chinese Generation Y, given the massive urbanization trends the country is experiencing). In such an "alternative MBA night school" program, the employees could, on the one hand, exercise their leadership skills in a corporate CSR project (i.e., in a "safe", case study-like environment), while being virtually coached through the project by a senior leader in the global HQ – providing the employee with the link back to both business teachings, corporate culture and knowledge.

Development reward and recognition

The corporate reward system needs to be increasingly locally implemented, ensuring a link to the asset management mindset and local specificities. There needs to be a compensation-and-benefits market competitiveness. However, it is questionable how long companies can sustain the recent upward wage spiral that has occurred in China and Russia. To supplement the compensation and benefits bedrock, the people assets need to be developed and "protected" using a number of local cultural insights, as discussed above in the four-level retention model.

Additionally, linked directly to development, there needs to exist a personal ownership of developers with their own "clientele" – and an interest in their development (which will in turn help develop the managers themselves). As an employee becomes more experienced, they are "rewarded" with more people responsibility. And finally, again linking back to the strategic intent of development, the internal performance and reward system needs to reflect this – in some cases allowing the "soft" results to count more than hard numbers in annual performance reviews.

BUILD AND TRAIN YOUR OWN TALENT

More and more companies realize that one of the critical success factors for future development is to build, train and nurture internal talent pools from scratch. Finding already trained talent outside your organization is difficult and expensive. One regional CEEMEA executive illustrated this point well in a recent conversation:

> "We simply stopped buying into the idea that the talent in emerging markets is scarce. It is scarce if you are looking for someone out there who is ready made. What we realized is that we can train our own talent and build our own permanent supply because there are bright and hard-working people throughout emerging markets. We look for the right attitudes, right psychological profiles, and then we train them from scratch in our internal 'university'. Most trainees are like sponges, they absorb everything quickly, and want to achieve. We see them as rough diamonds that we must invest in. So when people tell me that they

can't find good locals in Saudi, I tell them most of our internal staff in Saudi Arabia are Saudis because we created them."

Several companies that I work with have created incredibly well-oiled training engines for new employees, who sometimes have very modest educational backgrounds. One executive cites an example of a man with no education who was hired as a truck driver to physically deliver products to remote retail outlets. Ten years later and after many training programs, he has been promoted to run the whole country set-up for this consumer goods firm.

Any firm who wants to be a major player in emerging markets must allocate enough resources to build, train and nurture staff in every country – including those places where conventional prejudices suggest the people are "bad", "lazy" or "incompetent", or where there is supposedly a big shortage of talent.

INVEST IN HIGH-END LEADERSHIP TRAINING BECAUSE GOOD MANAGERS ARE NOT ENOUGH

There is a strong consensus among senior executives that emerging markets environment is so complicated, and will continue to be in the future, that having only good managers in an organization is simply not enough to achieve growth targets, to motivate people in good and bad times, to build teams and to work across corporate silos in multiple geographies.

In addition to having people who thrive on creating something, there must also be great leaders. Companies should therefore invest more and more in leadership training, but not just of any kind. Organizations that are constantly at the cutting edge of leadership research and training (such as the Center for Creative Leadership) can provide a huge depth of experience in working with major firms globally and regionally. It is not enough anymore to use a small, local leadership training outfit that does not have wide support in terms of cutting edge leadership research and top-notch, global trainers.

BUILD AND MENTOR YOUR COUNTRY-LEVEL SUCCESSION POOLS

In the future, all country level organizations will be run by locals or those "foreigners" who have been there so long they are almost seen as locals. Expats will be a thing of the past. Companies who look to the future are proactively mentoring and building local succession pools of very promising individuals who will one day be able to take on senior leadership positions. This has become a very systematic exercise that is transforming the way organizations function.

The knowledge transfer from mentors and expats is something that is increasing at an unprecedented speed. At the same time, companies are trying to ensure that those highly-trained, hand-picked individuals are also taken care of in terms of extra retention incentives.

> "We consider people in the succession pools in countries around the world as pure gold dust," says one regional director, "so much so that we have broken all internal rules when it comes to putting in

place packages that tie them into our corporate future. Over the last two years, only 3% have actually left, and we consider this a major success of our retention approach. One of our major competitors dismantled their succession pool in emerging markets because a new UK based CEO thought this was useless. I think he is a complete fool and that is good for us."

ALIGN INCENTIVES WITH LONG-TERM GOALS AND MARKET SHARE GAINS

This should be a global exercise for all companies that wish to have a strong international business. It is a good approach for abandoning the unhelpful obsession with quarterly earnings. It supports the build-up of sustainability of results. It is no use having a desire to build strong market positions in the future if market share gains and delivery over three-to-five year horizons is not part of the standard KPI (key performance indicators).

TESTING AND TRAINING CREATIVITY IN ORGANIZATIONS

> Discovery consists of looking at the same thing as everyone else and thinking something different.
>
> —Albert von Szent-Györyi, Nobel Prize for Physics winner

CREATIVITY IS ESSENTIAL AT THE INDIVIDUAL AND ORGANIZATIONAL LEVEL – TEST IT AND TRAIN IT

If a company wants to be better at innovation than others, it must have creative employees. Those companies that manage this process well in the next few years will be the huge winners in emerging markets. First, it is good to test job candidates to see how creative they are. Second, it is good to test existing employees to find out how creative they are. And third, it is important to provide training to employees because creativity skills can be developed. Most corporate staff use the logical/analytical left side of the brain in day-to-day work. Companies should train their staff and leaders on how to engage the creative right side of the brain more. In these challenging times for developing business in emerging markets, all grey cells should be running full speed together. Companies with ideas, out-of-the-box approaches and flexible minds are likely to navigate emerging markets with more success than others.

Creativity is defined as *"...the ability to produce or bring into existence something new by a course of action; to produce through imaginative skill"*. Rickards (1985) also defines creativity as *"...the personal discovery process, partially unconscious, leading to new and relevant insights ... through escape from mental stuckness"*. Creativity requires an in-depth knowledge of a subject (an intrinsic immersion in one's field) and an ability to make new connections.

Innovation comes as a by-product of insights and creative thinking. Innovation drives growth and new opportunities in different markets. Only those organizations that are constantly developing new products for their customers will survive the upcoming turbulent future.

Companies must appreciate the fact that almost everything done today in emerging markets involves new ways of thinking, resolving new sets of problems or generating novel ideas. Organizations ought to master creative thinking and its important by-product – innovation – to survive, but some corporations rarely put this on their list of priorities. Creative leaders, being more entrepreneurial, visionary, and resilient when under stress, use the power of their imagination, analogies, powerful allegories, or storytelling to inspire others' ideas and work, and calm their employees in times of turbulence, ambiguity, change and uncertainty. They create a competitive edge for their companies by responding positively when facing difficulties, and inspiring the same behaviour in their subordinates.

Creativity is a starting point of innovation and companies must ensure they have a system in place to build it and nurture it in all offices around the world. Through more creativity and innovation, corporations can better harness and find ways to market newfound products, materials and technology; have more exciting missions, techniques, concepts and processes; and better match products to clients' wants and needs.

Be aware that new ideas do not appear by chance. Isaac Newton once exclaimed: "How I was able to discover the law of gravity? By thinking of it continuously!" Thus training and organizational support brings powerful results. Research shows that creativity, including creative problem solving and generating novel, useful ideas, can be learned and nurtured on both an individual and organizational level.

Companies must assess personal and corporate levels of creativity and innovation potential in order to realize what their current strengths are and which developmental areas they should be improving. One of the most widely used and most comprehensive, holistic instruments for testing the creativity of job candidates, existing staff and organizations is the *Creativity and Innovation Pulse survey* (CIP survey®), which measures the creativity potential of both individuals and organizations. Through corporate players' responses, organizations obtain guidance on where and how to focus on increasing creativity from within (for more about this, contact: antonija.pacek@globalsuccessadvisors.eu). The key is to use the instrument first and then follow up with training to close creativity and innovation gaps.

Tapping into creativity and increasing innovation potential

- Unlearn personal strategies that hinder your creative expression (such as an inner critique or belief that "I'm not a creative person" – thereby creating a negative self-fulfilling prophecy).
- Use more analogies, associations and metaphors to open a road to your creative and innovative self.
- Question more often assumptions and beliefs.
- Improvise more often in order to easier adapt to change and turbulent situations.
- Find your own place for generating stimulating ideas.
- Tap more into your right brain hemisphere (which is more intuitive, imaginative, visual, spontaneous, art producing/appreciating, emotional) and be aware that we need both the left and right hemispheres working in tandem to produce most outstanding practical ideas, problem resolutions or new

processes or products. Our logical left hemisphere is very adequate for logical, rational thinking, but this is not enough for creativity.
- Know that there are many techniques for increasing personal creativity and innovation, but each of us will find our personal preference for a few of those techniques.
- Ask yourself often "what if" instead of "things should be this way…".
- Force yourself to come up with more than one solution!
- Be prepared to make mistakes (T.J. Watson, founder of IBM said, "If you want to increase your success rate, double your failure rate.")
- Make connections or associations between dissimilar subjects or areas.
- Think positively and expect excellent outcomes, as this opens up your mind to produce more, better and for a wider market (a lot of research proves this – for instance, Seligman's work).

Nurturing creativity and innovation
- Have creativity and innovation as the strategic focus of your organization.
- Allow your employees to mutually share their ideas as much as possible – build a participative atmosphere (great ideas are usually built from a variety of diverse sources).
- Encourage flexibility.
- The leadership needs to respect diversity and different employees' ideas (don't verbally 'kill' or punish through harsh remarks ideas that seem novel or different).
- Stimulate new ideas and problem solving: provide employees

with a creative room in which they can generate individually or brainstorm as a team (e.g., Google is well known for having such spaces in their organization, with various toys, musical instruments, table tennis, and material to write down ideas, as well as other props for inspiring new thinking). Also bring in innovative speakers from the outside: offer workshops with an out-of-the-box methodology, such as art-based inspirational learning.

- Put in place operating channels through which good ideas can be implemented.
- Give freedom for open self-expression – do not allow new ideas to be choked.

SEND SOME OF YOUR EMERGING MARKETS STAFF TO OFFICES IN THE DEVELOPED WORLD

To shake things up a little in slow-growing developed markets, many companies are increasingly promoting their best staff in emerging markets to key leadership positions in developed geographies. Many managers whom I know well and who originate from emerging markets are often shocked when they see how slow and fat some of the developed organizations are. One CEO said to me:

> "We are doing more of this cross breeding. In our developed world organizations we often do not notice anymore how awfully inefficient we have become – how overstaffed we are for what we actually deliver. These guys from emerging markets come in and

immediately see the big inefficiency gaps, because they are so used to the lean and mean emerging markets business environment. So it is a good thing to shake things up. At the same time, we must make sure that we are culturally sensitive. This exercise is also important for the future of the company. Some of these guys might one day do my job – so they must gain exposure to the developed world, too."

CONTINUOUSLY UP-SKILL ALL YOUR STAFF

Extraordinary times call for extraordinary staff. Only those firms that keep training their local employees at all levels and in all geographies will be able to cope with volatile economies and fast moving competition.

Chapter 5

ACQUISITIONS AS A WAY TO GROW

What if everything is an illusion and nothing exists? In that case, I definitely overpaid for my carpet.

—Woody Allen

ACADEMIC RESEARCH AND RESEARCH of various consulting firms over the years show that most mergers and acquisitions (M&A) deals do not always bring all the benefits they were supposed to bring to buyers. On average some 60% of transactions end up with some kind of problem, and the percentage rises in emerging markets.

I am still astonished by the speed of certain transactions prior to the crisis. One now retired deputy CEO of a large European bank told me over lunch in 2007 that they bought one bank in Central Eastern Europe with only one week of due diligence, although paying hundreds of millions of euros. He said they feared one of their competitors was going to get there first. Less than a year later, they discovered major problems in the accounts and had to absorb a massive write off. He later told me that the organic route to building that market share would have been much cheaper.

STRATEGIC CONSIDERATIONS

I have been observing M&A transactions of major multinationals in emerging markets for 20 years and the underlying issues have not changed over that time. Transactions largely go bad or do not bring value if companies rush the due diligence process and/or if they underestimate the cost and complexities of post-acquisition restructuring. If anything, this last global crisis has been good in one sense. Companies now take more time and are more careful about how they evaluate targets and how they assess earnings potential. In other words, the due diligence process is more rigorous and robust – and that is exactly what it should be. In addition, companies must remember that sometimes you have to walk away from a potentially bad deal, even if a huge amount of time was invested in it and it became somebody's internal "baby".

There is an increasingly important legal reason for more careful due diligence. "There is a greater awareness of directors' liability in case acquisitions go bad. Conducting superficial due diligence could be seen as gross negligence," says Dieter Spranz from Wolf Theiss law firm in Vienna.

There is, however, a need for due diligence to develop from merely filling in the pre-prepared checklists and demanding huge volumes of data to be transferred, a process which can try the patience of both buyers and sellers. The winners in the acquisition process are those buyers who are able to assess precisely the risks they need to cover and consider the most practical way to assess the volume and nature of those risks, and then make or reject an investment decision. A risk-focused approach, based on experience of the relevant market, is the only way to perform robust due diligence that has the best chance of protecting an investment.

DRIVING FORCES

In the future, there will be two big drivers of acquisition transactions in emerging markets. One stream will be transactions where multinationals buy their local competitors and/or emerging market multinationals. The second major stream will be acquisitions of country- or region-based operations of major multinationals as they pull out of certain geographies.

First, many local companies and emerging market multinationals have developed what multinationals seek: good market shares and well-established brands in certain countries. Often, these brands are active in other than premium segments and therefore fit the strategic aim of most multinationals to compete in multiple market segments in as many geographic areas around the world. Many of these transactions will be purely strategic and done for competitive reasons, such as: we want to remove the competitor that is stealing away our premium customers from the market. We also do not want to have our multinational competitors buying this local firm. These are all powerful reasons for companies to proactively manage their acquisition strategies and to create acquisition teams that seek out appropriate targets around the world. Major multinationals, considering their cash reserves, will be the major drivers of such acquisitions.

Second, competitive pressures are so large in almost all markets around the world that many multinationals will simply not be able to retain a share in a profitable way. All companies that do not follow the guidelines in this book will be vulnerable in the future, will lose market share and expose themselves to aggression from market leaders. "We have calculated that all players who have less than a 10% market share in our industry will not be able to stay in most emerging markets. It is a matter of time before we have to pull out," says an executive from the retail industry. The market leaders who focus on building sustainable business will eventually want to take over the assets of those who are leaving as markets consolidate. This is obviously not possible for all sectors, but it will be a major trend in certain sectors going forward.

Other types of transaction will include:
a) Emerging market multinationals buying aggressively in other emerging markets. The number of such transactions is increasing rapidly and will probably continue in the future.
b) In areas and times of economic slowdowns, the number of distressed M&A activity will always rise. This is the case in big parts of Central Eastern Europe today, for example.
c) When banks pull the plug on local players and force them into selling. As bank lending in some parts of the world tightens in the next few years, the number of such transactions will also increase.
d) Transactions driven by the so-called global "carve-outs" – companies selling business units or assets that no longer fit the core model or are underperforming relative to their other businesses.

e) Privatization driven transactions, as many governments go into a savings mode and are desperate for revenues that will plug budget deficits and reduce public debts.

f) Companies being put up for sale by private equity firms. Many private equity firms are coming under pressure from their lenders. They are now being forced to refinance their debts on stricter terms. One way out is to sell some holdings and realise their investments.

g) Private equity firms will also continue to buy companies very aggressively and then trying to resell them to multinationals. They are often faster to acquire targets than multinationals and this is why I urge my clients to set up very proactive internal acquisition teams rather than later overpay for companies previously acquired by private equity firms.

Globally, multinational buyers feel they have navigated through the crisis very well – many are sitting on sizeable and, in some cases, record cash accumulations as a result of massive cost cutting and efficiency drives in the immediate aftermath of the crisis. Many firms are using this cash to repurchase their shares (as a way to grow the infamous earnings-per-share), but needless to say many corporate eyes are on strategic acquisitions, notably in emerging markets. And this is how it should be. Many of these companies are seeking, through acquisitions, to expand their product portfolio not only in the premium segments (multinationals' usual playground), but also in the middle of the segmentation pyramid, where price points are lower but future growth potential is bigger.

In addition to having strong balance sheets, many multinationals are using the opportunity to raise some cheap financing at the moment either through corporate bond issues (increasingly also denominated in emerging markets' local currencies) or loans. Some of that money is now being used to drive growth through acquisitions, although the overall attitude is still strongly focused on cash preservation (largely because of economic uncertainties in the US, Western Europe and Japan). Banks are generally keen to work with multinationals that are looking to make acquisitions in emerging markets. They see multinationals as good customers and money is usually made available.

In the years before the crisis, private equity companies (with their access to incredibly large loans) were beating many multinationals in the fight for various emerging market firms. But high leverage is largely dried up and it is now cash-rich multinationals that should have an upper hand in terms of getting deals done and beating private equity competition. The next few years will offer multinationals a rare window of opportunity.

But, private equity firms have stepped up the effort and are accelerating the number of deals. "We have seen private equity firms using their aggression and deal know-how to push themselves proactively back into the M&A market," says one investment banker in Zurich. Also, there is a growing number of emerging market-owned private firms that have become sizeable players, have gone public and/or raised cash through corporate bond issues. The ambition of such firms is to go at least regional, and many are now scouting for distressed M&A opportunities all across emerging markets.

ACQUISITIONS

Below we look at important lessons gained during acquisitions in emerging markets and consider what successful companies have done to avoid acquisitions going wrong.

- Some executives think that buying companies in emerging markets sometimes resembles walking through a minefield without a mine detector. There are so many unknowns and only companies willing to equip themselves appropriately will actually succeed in performing good enough due diligence.
- Acquisitions often fail to add value to buying companies in the developed world, as numerous studies have shown. Making them work in emerging markets is even more difficult.
- Growth by acquisition is quicker but riskier than organic growth. Companies need to evaluate whether an acquisition is more cost-effective than organic growth for achieving a desired market position.
- An acquisition should offer clear advantages over achieving the same objectives through organic growth. Many companies feel that if there is no brand name, market share or strategic competitive advantage to a purchase in an emerging market, then it is probably better not to risk being involved in an acquisition.
- Companies should think hard and see clear advantages before embarking on an acquisition in a difficult market. And once they decide on an acquisition route, they must be extraordinarily careful with due diligence.

Acquiring companies in emerging markets is exceptionally complex, and underestimating this complexity is dangerous. A surprising

Acquiring companies in emerging markets is exceptionally complex, and underestimating this complexity is dangerous. number of very large companies still make mistakes in the acquisition process. Those mistakes are largely linked to poorly planned and executed due diligence before the purchase and/or poor assessment of post-acquisition challenges and costs. Some mistakes can cause almost irreparable damage to the business; others are less lethal but cause disruptions, delays and disappointing results.

When considering an acquisition strategy in emerging markets, companies should ask several additional questions:

- Do we have solid internal expertise to acquire in emerging markets?
- Are we in a position or are we willing to have a dedicated, proactive internal acquisitions team that will search for, and engage in, emerging market acquisitions?
- Are we aware how complex the due diligence process can be and the issues we need to address during the due diligence process?
- Are we aware that we must get help from locally-based advisors (foreign or locally owned)?
- Are the managers in a target company that we value for or against acquiring? This is important because internal resistance may undermine an acquisition.
- Do we have a clear strategy and plan as to how we want to run the business being acquired post-acquisition, and is this linked to our due diligence plan?
- Do we really know the individuals with whom we are "getting into bed with" as a result of this transaction?

It is crucial to ask difficult internal questions and then later be proactive in seeking out acquisition opportunities and executing transactions. There are few great acquisition targets in emerging markets and the competition to buy them is often fierce; prices can be surprisingly high and rising. It is often the fast firms that buy companies, not the big ones, so you need to identify and approach the best targets early. Working fast but still doing a thorough due diligence is a challenge that is best handled by having a dedicated internal team that can co-ordinate financial, legal, tax, HR and other advisors. Assigning a manager to lead acquisitions who has other duties often results in a lack of necessary speed and focus. Needless to say, local presence is a great help in securing speed in due diligence and the actual transaction, as well as in post-acquisition restructuring.

A target evaluation in emerging markets must address the following areas.

RESEARCH THE BACKGROUND OF THE TARGET COMPANY

This part of the evaluation should focus on describing the acquisition target in the past and present, as well as its strategy. It is important to know the acquired company's strategic strengths and weaknesses.

EXAMINE THE TARGET COMPANY'S MARKETS, PRODUCTS AND MARKETING

A buyer obviously needs an in-depth understanding of the business's products or services. It is also crucial to determine the market share potential of the business's products, particularly when buying market share is the primary motive for the acquisition.

In doing this, market developments and trends should be taken into account.

Here are some important questions a buyer should answer:
a) What is the product portfolio of the target company and what are its market shares? How have market shares moved up or down in the past and why? Has there been any sizeable market share deterioration recently?
b) What are the USP (unique selling proposition), pricing history and profit margins? What will drive demand for products and their prices in the future? What is the risk of future price wars?
c) What is the product positioning and is it correct in terms of new market needs?
d) How do competitors, distributors and consumers perceive the product and its quality? Conduct primary research and detect any dissatisfaction and negative brand perceptions early.
e) Is there scope to improve the quality and service and how much will that cost?
f) Is this market segment in which a target operates under pressure or shrinking relative to other segments? Is it cyclical and how long are the cycles? Which market segments are actually growing?
g) How large should marketing and advertising expenses be to accelerate demand and earnings in the future?

PAY SPECIAL ATTENTION TO FINANCIAL DUE DILIGENCE
Financial projections should be based on careful analysis of which assumptions are sound and what will drive demand. Future earnings

potential is what matters. When examining the business's financial statements, buyers should keep in mind that these are frequently ambiguous and unreliable and that accounting standards can differ from international norms.

The financial due diligence should help in assessing the value of the business, but there will almost always be disagreements between buyer and seller as to what the company is worth. Past performance is not a useful indicator for business valuation in emerging markets, so buyers try to make the price an aspect of the business's earnings potential. Sellers rarely agree with this valuation and frequently put higher values based on past sales and/or often place very high values on their fixed assets.

Price is not necessarily the principal issue in reaching agreement on an acquisition. Treatment of management and workers often plays an important role when it comes to state-owned deals in particular, as do promises of further investments and on-the-job training programs.

DETERMINING MARKET VALUE

Determining market value is not easy for a number of reasons:

a) **Available information is not necessarily reliable.**
Many companies are not listed on any stock exchange so valuing them is similar to valuing a closely held business in the developed world. Even if a company is listed on a stock exchange, not all exchanges are well regulated.

b) **Past earnings are not necessarily a guide to future performance.**

Earnings forecasts should be crucial in determining value. But getting a true financial picture of the past is tricky. Past earnings are distorted by new (and future) market conditions that will, or may have been, less competitive than they are now. The implications for future cash flows are enormous. It is essential to investigate how much the company's earnings may be boosted by monopoly privileges, low-interest loans, privileged access to government contracts, subsidised rents, lack of compliance or other government help. By removing these factors from cash-flow calculations, a more realistic picture emerges. This sounds sensible, but how do you go about evaluating the cash flow generating ability of companies that have never operated without subsidies, subtle government protection or appalling lack of compliance? All you can do is carry out due diligence in order to fully understand the drivers of future sales.

c) **Many buyers have found that balance sheets reveal questionable information.**

The problem is that assets, especially equipment, are often overvalued in a firm's official financial statements. Furthermore, in many countries assets often have longer lives and lower depreciation rates than in the developed world. You may find that certain assets have never depreciated. But assets are worth only what they are able to produce, and this should be the basis for valuation. If assets can only produce an outdated product poorly, they are worthless – a fact that local sellers find hard to believe.

d) **It is crucial to check whether listed receivables are enforceable.**

In many countries the quality of the legal system is poor and trying to enforce payment of receivables through the legal process is often a long, difficult and expensive exercise. Signed contracts promising new production orders are another potential trap. They should not be accepted at face value; investigations should be made into how likely they are to materialise. The system of inter-company invoicing and recording of receivables is slow and inefficient in some emerging markets. Unpaid invoices pile up and demands for payment become impossible to enforce.

e) **Ask question about any company-to-company borrowing.**

Given tight credit conditions in some emerging markets and still high interest rates, local companies can have difficulties obtaining bank loans. This was certainly the case in the past and many emerging markets firms often borrowed from each other. Extreme care should be taken during due diligence to try to determine the level of inter-enterprise debt. Many such debts are never recorded on a balance sheet.

f) **Investigate any tax and social security liabilities.**

An important part of the financial audit is to check for any tax liabilities. Many firms have discovered that their acquisition targets had not paid tax or social security for years, thus creating a large, potential liability and inflating their results. Some firms have been pursued by the tax authorities after the acquisition to pay owed tax. The risk of this happening should be avoided by thorough due diligence. In some countries in the region, SME targets tend to hire individuals as sub-contractors instead of as employees. It is necessary to mitigate the risk in such cases by estimating the impact of any tax liability on business.

g) **Pro forma adjustments are important**

"Make pro forma adjustments to EBITDA to reflect the value of a full-time CEO. Owner-managers sometimes do not take any compensation, or take too much. Other pro-forma adjustments need to be made regarding equipment, factories or rented offices if pricing seems questionable. The same caution and adjustments need to be applied to plausibility of items that the target management claims are non-business related," reported one M&A advisor from KPMG.

h) **Assess whether a balance sheet really reflects all the liabilities of a business.**

The ability of the company to repay its debt service schedule is something that companies must take into account when making assumptions about the future.

One note of caution: beware of a target management that claims its financial results are audited. Check who the auditor is. Make sure that the audit was done by a credible firm. Several of our clients have discovered that many small audit firms are little more than a back-room local who happens to have an audit license and is, sometimes, a friend of the owner of the audited firm.

THINK ABOUT LONG-TERM EARNINGS STREAMS

Companies whose senior management is supportive of long-term business development are sometimes prepared to pay well over current value. They are more concerned about what the purchase can bring in terms of long-term earnings streams and what it means strategically – if it captures, for example, an important local brand and thus limits the competition's room for manoeuvre.

Nevertheless, a buyer should try to create a business plan based on future profit estimates, taking into account all the uncertainties involved, and measure it against the price being asked for the business. The value of a candidate as a going concern depends on future cash flows and earnings, discounted back to the present using an appropriate discount rate. When trying to determine the appropriate discount rate, it is necessary to make adjustments for distortions created by monopolies, subsidies, lack of compliance and past (perhaps now irrelevant) trading links. This is, of course, a subjective process, but some provisions should be made.

Further problems arise when trying to make realistic assumptions on future performance. This is especially hard when trying to predict a target company's sales and profits in five years' time. Emerging markets can change rapidly for a number of reasons, such as the threat of economic crisis, changing consumer habits and inflow of new domestic or international competitors.

UNDERSTANDING THE TECHNOLOGY

Make sure you understand the manufacturing processes and technology of the target company before acquiring. The main goal of this part of the investigation is to estimate the investment that will be required after acquisition to integrate the acquired business into a global manufacturing system and to achieve desired standards of productivity and quality. An assessment should also be made to determine the ease and cost of expanding the facility for any future increases in demand.

The investigation should answer some of the following questions:

a) What are the current manufacturing processes and the capacity and state of equipment? How productive is the facility?

b) How are supply channels organised? What has been the behaviour of supply channel participants? What are the current supply problems?

c) If there are any problems with the supply of components? Can these be solved? What is the local supplier base of manufacturing components like? Will we have to persuade our global suppliers to invest nearby?

d) What are the availability and prices of raw materials? How are those likely to behave in the next five years?

e) Are there R&D facilities and researchers that could be integrated into the buyer's regional and global strategy?

f) Have management made consistent investments into its manufacturing equipment over the last few years (especially during the crisis years) or is there a capital–expenditure gap that will have to be funded by the buyer in the near future?

COMPLIANCE DUE DILIGENCE

Do not close any deals until you have thoroughly completed the compliance due diligence process.

One of our CEEMEA Business Group members who is in a B2B industrial sector has recently spent over a year doing a very thorough due diligence. However, he overlooked a crucial point:

how sales were generated in the CIS markets. The deal had already gone through several phases of internal approval and was getting ready for the final approval process. A tip-off from a sales director from the target company warned the buyer of the fact that over the years, most sales had been done by paying substantial bribes to managing directors of customer companies. The managing director of the multinational company then accompanied the sales director on a few sales trips and warned that in the future no bribes would be paid when the new buyer took over. All managing directors of local firms then said they would have to look for new suppliers. After this experience and several million spent on due diligence, the multinational company walked away from the deal.

It is essential that buyers always check a whole stream of compliance issues, and particularly how sales were generated in the past. Strip away bribe paying from the equation and you might be buying a completely useless, unprofitable company.

IF YOU ARE BUYING A MANUFACTURING PLANT, DO NOT FORGET TO DO ENVIRONMENTAL DUE DILIGENCE

In some highly polluting sectors, this should be the first due diligence step. Companies often find environmental damage on site. The audit should establish the extent of any damage and more importantly, indicate how the liability can be contractually avoided. Several companies have made acquisitions and have later been asked by local authorities to clean up the damage that was there before a purchase. Buyers should make it clear before a purchase that they will not be held responsible for any existing environmental damage.

LEGAL DUE DILIGENCE

A legal due diligence typically includes the following (the list below is a brief and high-level list of topics provided by law firm Wolf Theiss):

a) **Corporate:** Proper legal existence and registration of the company; ownership of shares (including trusteeships and silent participations); encumbrances over shares; liabilities and other legal issues relating to corporate restructurings in the past (contributions in kind, mergers, spin-offs, transformations, etc); obligations under shareholder agreements, joint ventures or alike agreements (restrictions on share transfers, such as pre-emption rights, approval requirements, tag-along drag-along rights, funding obligations, voting restrictions, etc); legal issues relating to share capital increases/decreases or other capital measures of the past.

b) **Financial matters:** Liabilities and other legal issues in relation to loan and credit agreements, security agreements, guarantees, surety, patronage statements, comfort letters and other financing instruments, intra group financing and clearing agreements (cash pooling), government subsidies.

c) **Compliance and regulatory:** Status of compliance with laws, regulations and codes of conduct (under laws dealing with anti-corruption, anti-trust, competition, corporate governance, commercial data protection, etc); existence and status of permits and licenses necessary to carry out the business operations and to own, use, lease and operate the properties, installations, buildings and assets.

d) **Material agreements:** Specific provisions in important agreements (with important customers or suppliers), such as relating to change of control, warranties and other liabilities, non-compete provisions, durations and termination of commercial terms upon request.

e) **Employment agreements:** With managing directors, pension schemes, benefit schemes, employee stock options, profit-sharing plans, company works agreements and unusual or onerous clauses in general employment guarantees, obstacles in relation to redundancy measures (if relevant).

f) **Real property:** Legal titles to own, lease or otherwise use land and buildings (land registry extracts, purchase agreements, lease agreements, easements, superstructure agreements, building right agreements, etc) and potentially onerous legal aspects arising thereafter.

g) **Other material assets:** Legal titles to own, lease or otherwise use other material assets.

h) **Intellectual property:** Titles and limitations to trademarks, patents, patterns, copyrights, or similar rights used by the company; violations of third party intellectual rights.

i) **Litigation:** Status and relevance of potential or pending legal, arbitral or administrative proceedings.

In practice, a legal due diligence checklist is much more detailed and typically tailored to the specifics of the relevant target.

INCLUDE ORGANIZATIONAL STRUCTURE AND HUMAN RESOURCES IN DUE DILIGENCE

"Unfortunately, in my experience the 'human' aspect of pre-M&A activity is largely neglected across emerging markets," says Mark Hamill, Global Managing Director of Spengler Fox, an

HR advisory and executive search firm. He adds: "Evaluating and understanding the talent you have and the talent you need to make a deal successful – i.e., talent audits – are becoming embedded more and more in deals in emerging markets."

It is important to understand the existing management structure and human resources in order to successfully change it if need be. The due diligence process must look at the costs and requirements of reorganization, since without substantial reorganization most acquisitions are doomed to fail. It is also important to know who the important people in the organization are, at both management and supervisory level. Will there be extra costs if these people are kept on? Are they likely to leave? What would keep them at the company? Acquisitions often fail because some key employees are unwilling to work with new employers and decide to leave. If new structures and systems are imposed, will these be in sharp contrast to the existing systems in the target company? If significant work has to be done, this will have to be planned for and executed during post-acquisition restructuring.

Recent work by Spengler Fox reveals that the level of engagement with HR partners and innovative talent consultants is significantly lower than it should be, both before and after due diligence. Mark Hamill says: "But we have built a talent pool of relevant advisors and non-executive directors who get engaged pre- and post-acquisition and give advice on deal viability, deal value, post-acquisition issues and developing the strategy to drive the business forwards."

According to multinational buyers, owners/CEOs of SME targets make all final decisions, and such organizations rarely have a management information system, since all the key information is in the owner's head. Buyers must understand that sometimes it is the owner who is the bottleneck for growth – buyers must take appropriate steps with the owner in order to fulfill the future potential of the company.

ASSESS THE ROLE THAT PERSONAL RELATIONSHIPS PLAY

Many companies have found out too late that the strong sales of the company they have acquired were the result of close personal relationships between the former owner or his sales staff and clients. When an international company takes a firm over, the people who have nurtured these relationships may well leave, which can leave an acquisition that seemed so promising looking distinctly shaky. Again, this is a matter of due diligence. If those sales relationships are crucial, the company should either seek to recruit the people who have those relationships and follow the organic route to growth, or devise a strategy to keep them in the event of an acquisition (which would involve talking to them well in advance to determine what would persuade them to stay).

RESTRUCTURING AND INTEGRATION – BE AWARE OF WHAT IS WAITING FOR YOU

Post-acquisition restructuring in emerging markets is often costly and time-consuming. Integrating different working attitudes and cultures is always difficult, but most emerging market businesses require a substantial overhaul if they are to become an integral and successful part of the buyer's company. One of the most complicated issues in post-acquisition restructuring is trying to increase productivity. This typically involves laying off employees. From the beginning, the buying company should pursue a positive public relations campaign and communicate with opinion leaders among the workforce.

If employees turn against the deal after it is completed, the company can suffer immense difficulties. In many countries acquisition contracts can stipulate no lay-offs for a certain period, usually ranging from one to three years. Multinationals may be opposed to such agreements, but many recognize that they are an important way of showing sensitivity to local public opinion and therefore sometimes agree to these conditions.

Keeping a factory over-manned for some time may seem wasteful but it has some advantages. It helps avoid negative publicity. It gives time to help those who will be laid off – for example, through offering incentives to those who volunteer for early retirement. But buyers should be aware in advance of the cost of closing the deal. You may find scores of workers listed as employees in the books who were registered merely to have time counted towards their pension and to receive social and health benefits. Thorough due diligence should identify the number of such workers.

Another reason for giving short-term employment guarantees is that many firms need time to restructure the acquired business. This allows them to assess individual employees and decide which ones they want to keep and which they do not need when the guarantee has runs its term. Spinning off certain businesses and units is a way to improve efficiency and lower the headcount.

Another way to win over locals and workers is to create good outplacement and retraining programs for those who are not wanted. The message is clear: "We are not just kicking you out – we will help you acquire new skills and we will try to help you find work elsewhere. Also, once we reach our production targets and productivity starts to grow, we will need new people, and you will be the first ones we will look at." Such an attitude boosts the morale of those who stay because everyone likes to work for an employer who cares.

Ask any M&A consultant why acquisitions often fail and one of the top three responses will be poor post-acquisition restructuring and integration. Integration is a complex procedure. It involves keeping all retained employees focused, making sure the best people have good incentives to stay and identifying early any potential personnel conflicts. It also involves merging organizational cultures and structures and engaging new employees in new activities. A skilled integration manager should work closely with an external human resources consultancy specializing in integration issues. One of the most critical issues is to make sure that staff in the acquired company fully understand the objectives of the acquisition, the plan for the future and how it will be implemented.

Make sure that staff in the acquired company fully understand the objectives of the acquisition, the plan for the future and how it will be implemented.

Mark Hamill from Spengler Fox has experience in this area:

"We were recently retained to replace four out of five executive board members in an acquired firm who had walked out within three months of the deal being made. This left the firm in a precarious position with a highly fragile local team. The impact would have been significantly reduced had we been earlier engaged as a talent audit along with other HR solution tools. This would have yielded valuable information and allowed us to significantly reduce 'time to hire' and be prepared for a worst case scenario."

Chapter 6

TIPS FOR EXECUTIVE SURVIVAL AND ADVANCEMENT IN EMERGING MARKETS

> Just as I discovered the meaning of life, they changed it.
>
> —*George Carlin*

SURVIVING IN A LEADERSHIP position at a country, regional or international level is becoming more and more complicated. Tenures are shrinking. Global companies are impatient with those who do not deliver quickly and/or consistently. They are even more impatient with those who miss budget targets. In fact, my own little, unscientific tracking sheet of my clients who lost their positions in the last five years shows that they were more likely to lose the job for not hitting a budget or two than for almost any other "sin". Those that grew less but hit the budget usually survived. That is how strange the business world has become. But almost everyone now accepts it as normal. Based on observing typical corporate survivors over the last 20 years or so, I have collected a few words of sometimes amusing wisdom for executive survival and advancement in emerging markets. Here they are.

EMBRACE AND ACCEPT THE GROWTH STORY – OR AT LEAST WHOLE-HEARTEDLY PRETEND YOU DO

A year does not go by without people above you coming up with yet another "stepping up the effort" or "accelerated growth path" strategy. And for you it always feels like déjà vu. You can bet that, in particular, any newly appointed manager will give you some enormous stretch target, which they will expect you to deliver quickly. They want you to be involved, they want you to drive faster growth for your territory or business unit, and they want your full cooperation and agreement. They will come up with mega targets such as: "You are selling 100 units now but we want to increase this to 400 in three years. How will you do it? Give us your ideas. And do not tell us this is not possible. You are operating in an emerging market and it is a growth market, so why are we not booming here? Make business boom or we will find someone else to do it for us!"

If you need a job, you do not have much choice but to accept the growth *diktat*. You can think of leaving, but you should be under no illusion that it will be any different in other firms, since everyone is obsessed with finding more growth in emerging markets. If you think the growth they are proposing is impossible to achieve (so many executives do), continue to play along if you want to keep the job. If you are about to retire and you dislike the newly appointed manager, tell him to go to hell and take that early retirement. Or better still, promise you will deliver, fail and then retire. So that "asshole" above you will miss the budget. But if you actually enjoy growing the business in a fast paced manner (there are so many great managers that I know who genuinely do), then what can be better than some good position in an emerging markets environment where more and more sales growth is needed? Delivering consistently fast growth in emerging markets is just a way of life and it is not for everyone. Many executives that I know genuinely enjoy the fast pace and growth, but many are trying to navigate the waters with more caution, less energy and by faking they actually care.

In the end, even if you do not like the latest version of an "accelerated growth strategy" and you *still* care about the job, you and your team will still come up with numerous ideas as to how this can be achieved. And do not forget to tell the people above you how much you and your team enjoy doing this "accelerated growth" exercise. Never, ever show any doubt that this cannot be done. And do it with a smile. The people above you must know you as a "can do" guy who always has new ideas for the business. You will also need that smile for the second important exercise, called "managing expectations downwards". Because remember, the last thing you want to do is to accept the biggest stretch budget and then not deliver it.

One regional director I have known for years admits:

> "When I talk to my country managers about faster growth and stretch targets, I know most of them think I am an idiot and that the numbers I quote I do not believe myself. Just as they think I am an idiot, I think my global boss is an idiot for setting me such extreme stretch targets. I know my boss well so I

know he is not an idiot, but he thinks the CEO is an idiot for asking him to ask teams around the world to grow so fast. And the CEO probably thinks his board and shareholders are idiots for demanding so much. One can conclude we are nothing but a bunch of idiots working for extremely wealthy shareholders to make them even richer than they are. But such is life! We are now introducing more share options even at relatively low levels of the organization in emerging markets in order to have everyone feel like owners."

MANAGE EXPECTATIONS PROACTIVELY DOWNWARDS, ALL THE TIME

In a world when everyone above you always says, "Give me more", one of the most important managerial skills in emerging markets is to consistently manage expectations downwards. This is more easily done if you are seen as a "can do" guy who is wholeheartedly (or wholeheartedly pretending) to be the big advocate or supporter of accelerated growth. The ultimate purpose of managing expectations is to:

a) make sure you massage the stretch target downwards so that it really is achievable or even better, beatable; and

b) communicate upwards all possible things that can go wrong, especially those factors in the external environment over which you have little or no influence. That way, you at least have something on paper that says, "I told you this was not realistic."

Managing expectations is a fine balancing exercise. On one side you still have to be the "guy who loves growth", but on the other hand you must try to bring the original stretch targets down for at least two reasons. First, you are more likely to lose your job for missing a target than for almost any other reason. Second, you want the target to be as low as possible so you can beat it. The guys who progress upwards in corporations are those that consistently beat targets.

So how to do this? When you are doing faster growth preparation and planning, note all the potential issues that can go wrong with the plan. For example: we cannot grow fast in this market because we were planning to replace that bad distributor; we cannot grow fast in that market because we do not have any local presence; we cannot grow fast in that market because elections are upcoming, and usually around elections orders stop for four months; we cannot grow in this market because everyone says this currency will collapse within the next few months; we cannot grow in these markets unless we increase spending on our brand-building, and this will cost money so the profit target for the next few years will be lower; etc, etc. So while you are thinking about growth, consider seriously all the possible obstacles, country by country, that can derail the growth plan.

And after you present the good news about growth, you must warn people above you of all the things that threaten that plan. Here you have an inherent structural ally. No one above you wants to miss their own target so they have a vested interest in listening and absorbing the things that you identify as business risks. Remember that the person above you also has his own skin to protect and he does not want to miss the budget either. By listing all the risks, you are covering your back, but you are also giving ammunition to your boss to manage expectations of the people above him.

A good phrase to use during those corporate presentations is: "The opportunities are great, but no one wants to end up with an unrealistic target that we will all miss." Another good phrase to use is: "We do not want to promise too fast growth in year one until we create preconditions for faster growth for the three or five year plan."

Manage expectations continuously. For that you need to keep monitoring markets closely, try to anticipate things that can go wrong and try to anticipate any new risks on the horizon. And then it is all about communication, communication and communication. But do not complain first. Instead, be positive initially and then later talk about the risks.

MANAGE EXPECTATIONS ALL THE WAY TO THE TOP – BRING THE TOP GUYS OVER TO VISIT YOUR AREA

When corporate officers visit certain geographies they always get a dose of reality. They can see the opportunities and risks for themselves. Therefore, if a visit is organized well, your communications with them about the rate of growth and risks involved will be easier to explain. Those at the very top have to see what can go well and what can go wrong. Remember that your CEO also has to manage analysts', owners' and the board's expectations. He does not want to be the fool who has to repeatedly inform them that he missed quarterly growth targets.

Visits are also good because CEOs and top officers tend to ask a number of good questions and can bring a new perspective based on their long-standing experience. As a head of a geographic area, you do not want to invite the CEO only. Other top people have to be involved, too. If you argue for more resources or if you want to massage expectations down, there needs to be a broad group of people at the top who understand what you are saying and why you are saying it. It is no use just getting just the CEO on board. There will always be certain corporate officers who have specific prejudices about some areas or businesses, unless they see things for themselves.

Also, do not only take them only to the best hotel, top restaurants and in and out of meeting rooms. Make sure they visit your customers, as well as visit customers of your competitors to hear why they prefer your competitors (who knows, maybe they have a better product portfolio?). Prepare short, punchy material about your area, highlighting the pluses and minuses, and do this early enough so that they have time to absorb the message. Make sure your staff presents to them, too – not just you – then also take them to some poorer areas of the country so they can see that not everything is perfect. Also bring in an external authority to explain the economics and business trends of your area (outsiders are always trusted more).

When you present to them, make sure you are enthusiastic about growth, but realistic about risks. Make sure they see both sides of the coin very clearly. Make sure you present some new ideas and initiatives about growth. And most definitely prepare some benchmarking data that shows the level of penetration in your market. If for example, your competitors' sales in India are 5% of their global sales, and yours is only 2% of global sales, this usually means you have underpenetrated, thanks to a lack of upfront resources.

Demonstrate that your competitors are gaining share and offer explanations as to why (this usually boils down to superiority of resources). This is a key exercise if you are to approach them with the big question: "Can I have more resources in order to achieve higher growth?" Remember that it is much worse to end up with a big stretch budget without the resources to execute it properly. And I have seen over the years too many executives in this horrible trap, which rarely ends well for the responsible executive.

WORK ON REALISTIC AND SUSTAINABLE TARGETS

Although on the surface you are in the game of growing the top and bottom lines of the business, most executives will readily admit that the real game is to meet budgets if you want to survive, and beat budgets if you want to prosper. With that in mind, part of your energy has to be channeled into setting realistic growth targets for the market(s) that you are responsible for. In order to do this you must make sure you are monitoring economic developments regularly (or have an external organization helping you with this). You must assess all the things that can go wrong and footnote them on your budget spreadsheet ("I told our CEO that the currency might fall and that our business would suffer as

> **The real game is to meet budgets if you want to survive, and beat budgets if you want to prosper.**

a consequence."). Protect yourself by warning those above of you of the risks.

The hard reality is that targets should not only be realistic and in line with your resource allocation – they must also be *sustainable*. There is little gain for the prosperity of the business to have one great year, where you grow the bottom line superbly because you squeezed costs (which anyone can do), and then go into lower growth mode later. Goals should be sustainable year in and year out. Try to determine with your teams what is the sustainable growth rate for the top and bottom line for the next three to five years in each emerging market; examine the reasons why and make sure you communicate this upwards. More and more CEOs are interested in sustainable growth and this approach will resonate with them. Remember that your CEO will also prosper if he is seen as someone who delivers consistent growth over a longer period of time.

ALWAYS DISGUISE CERTAIN BUSINESS INITIATIVES FROM THE PEOPLE ABOVE YOU – HAVE AN UNOFFICIAL BUDGET

Always have some business up your sleeve that you can throw into a quarter or a year, something you have not reported upwards. This acts as a contingency – it is your career protection tool. This kind of contingency is useful to have in emerging markets because things rarely go according to plan: you lose some deals last minute, governments collapse, currencies depreciate, or whatever.

Consequently, you and your staff should always work on more projects and plans than you actually budget for. You should have an official budget and an unofficial one. Some smart executives I know well tell their subordinates that the unofficial budget is actually real so that everyone treats it with the utmost seriousness and focus. The logic here is simple: some sales from the unofficial budget won't come to fruition, so when these sales don't happen you will end up exactly where the lower official budget is.

Chapter 7

BEST PRACTICES FOR MEDIUM-SIZED FIRMS GOING REGIONAL OR GLOBAL

If you think you are too small to make an impact, try going to bed with a mosquito in the room.

—*Betty Reese*

THERE IS A GROWING NUMBER of medium-sized firms, largely coming from the developed world (but not exclusively), that are keen to expand their export business to neighboring countries, regionally or even globally. Many realize they have outgrown their domestic markets, and like larger firms they are trying to find growth elsewhere. Even small firms are increasingly looking outside (these tend to be very niche players or firms that can use technology to quickly sell their products anywhere on the planet). In this short chapter I will largely focus on medium-sized firms that have enough muscle for at least limited global expansion.

In recent years I have had the pleasure of interacting with many medium-sized firms who were keen on expanding their export business. Some of them actually originated from emerging markets and felt they had saturated their domestic market. In my work with them I realized that many were making critical mistakes when looking at how to expand their export business. Below is a list of dos based on my long-standing observations of how medium-sized firms became multinationals in the past.

UNDERSTAND THE MARKETS BEFORE YOU DO ANYTHING ELSE

You are not a big multinational, but you are also not a "mom-and-pop" shop. So you will have to invest in understanding markets upfront. Important issues include:

- market size and potential
- local consumers and customers
- economic outlook
- key aspects of the current and future business environment (including, for example, import duties, corruption, government policies towards business and legal frameworks)
- distribution dynamics and key players (including their ease or difficulties accessing financing)
- investigating all competitors and their pricing/products/operations
- the cost of properly building a brand

Almost every medium-sized firm that I have ever encountered has had some regrets in not understanding what they were getting into.

USE EXTREME CAUTION AND RESEARCH IN DEPTH WHEN PRIORITIZING WHERE TO GO FIRST

For medium-sized firms with limited resources it is extremely important to first enter markets that can offer the quickest returns. Those returns can be used to reinvest in those markets as well as provide investment to open up business in other countries. The research points I mentioned in the previous paragraph can be used to map potential markets and help pick the place that will bring the best return fastest.

FOCUS ON SUSTAINING THE BUSINESS, RATHER THAN A QUICK SELL

Most medium-sized companies appoint an export manager who is responsible for finding distributors in as many geographies as possible. They travel around, meet potential distributors and resellers, sign contracts and instigate first shipments. They are happy because business seems to be moving. However, they often experience a nasty surprise when local distributors call and cancel orders.

A typical conversation goes something like this:

Distributor: "Sorry, we are going to cancel the next order. It is not selling well. We have not even sold the last batch you shipped."

Export director: "What is going on? Is something happening with the economy that we are not aware of? Anything wrong with the product?"

Distributor: "No, no, everything is fine with the economy and the product, but few people know about it and therefore there is little demand…"

Export director: "But isn't your marketing campaign generating some demand?"

Distributor: "Well, to be honest, we've had some financial difficulties since the beginning of the year and had to delay the marketing campaign. We are

	actually not sure how much we can spend on it in the near future."
Export director:	"But in our contract you agreed to run regular marketing campaigns for us…"
Distributor:	"Sorry, we were not able to do so…"
Export director:	"But you are breaching the contract."
Distributor:	"Sorry, I can't hear you. The line is breaking up… hello, hello…"
Export director:	"Hello, hello, can you hear me…? Shit! Hello!"

When I present this short conversation in front of audiences it does get a lot of laughs because almost every export manager has experienced something similar in some shape or form.

Too many firms start a business in a developing market that either does not last (worst case) or does not grow well (best case). I always say to my medium-sized clients that it is better to focus on a fewer markets and do them properly than sign up a huge number of distributors in so many geographies. As with large firms, "fly-in, fly-out" management without focused brand-building on the ground does not work. This means developing in the new market all those same things you do in your home market: i.e., controlling and continuously investing in a marketing mix. This is the only way exporters can create what I call "staying power" in countries.

USE YOUR SMALLER SIZE TO BE MORE NIMBLE AND QUICKER THAN BIGGER COMPANIES

A number of my large clients increasingly cite stories of medium-sized firms gaining market share in emerging markets. They consider them annoying competitors because the big boys do not like to be beaten by small boys. But there is also respect for medium-sized firms' speed of decision making, ability to capture niches, ability to price attractively and offer high quality. These are the typical, inbuilt advantages that medium-sized firms can use in their battle with large and often inflexible corporate "tankers". I tell medium-sized firms to proactively and in detail map the activities of their larger competitors, including looking at their products and positioning. Such analysis usually reveals gaps in the strategy and approach of the larger players. The aim is to exploit those gaps aggressively.

SET UP REGIONAL OFFICES FIRST, COUNTRY OFFICES SECOND

Since the name of the game is to gain more control over business in order to make it longer lasting (while at the same time resources are more limited than in big firms), it is essential to open four or five small regional hubs in key emerging market regions. At the beginning these could truly be "one man and a dog" set-ups, but the purpose is get closer to distributors, to work with them, and to start looking at how brands can be developed in selected markets.

This is a better solution that having an export manager who, say, lives in Germany or Sweden, but spends his/her life on long-distance flights. Remoteness from distributors and consumers/customers is truly unhelpful. At least small regional hub offices provide some proximity to the action. Such regional hubs also contribute to firms learning about local markets and about future market and resource allocations.

Such offices are not a killer expense for medium-sized firms (even those smaller medium-sized firms that turn over something like US $100 million per year) and the pluses over time are enormous in terms of creating presence and consistent sales growth.

MAKE SURE YOU SELECT THE RIGHT PEOPLE TO RUN YOUR EXPORT BUSINESS AND INTERNATIONAL EXPANSION

Too many medium-sized firms just pick someone from the existing organization to develop their export business. Those individuals, although invariably capable and intelligent, are usually not the perfect candidates. Simply, they lack crucial international experience, since most of their professional and private lives have been spent in domestic (usually developed) markets.

Companies find that investing in people with the right experience in international business results in significantly faster and more consistent growth. It is an investment worth making. This applies not only to the head of exports, who sits in the headquarters, but also to people who co-ordinate distributors and control the business from regional or local hubs.

FOCUS TEST PRODUCTS AND SERVICES BEFORE GOING IN

A lot of good preparatory research can get you far in terms of understanding new markets, but talking to potential buyers before market entry can add completely new twists to the equation. Qualitative conversations tend to be enormously revealing in terms of assessing potential demand and the pitfalls ahead. The outlay is not enormous but the benefits are huge in terms of positioning the product correctly and in how you pitch it to the local buyers.

In case you need to go through retail outlets, it is worth talking to them to hear their opinions about your product, their expectations of you and their valuable views about the market.

PUT EXTRA FOCUS ON SMALL COUNTRIES WITH LESS COMPETITION

Many large players continue to focus on major markets. Competition is intense, with price wars escalating. The window of opportunity to enter and sustain the business is narrowing in large markets. However, many large players continue to be less focused on smaller countries. But competition is not as fierce there. Therefore, medium-sized firms should also assess smaller markets as part of a prioritization exercise.

LAST BUT NOT LEAST: APPLY THE LESSONS FROM THIS BOOK

HR lessons, marketing excellence tips (particularly those describing finding and working with distributors) and strategic advice for sustainability should all be, ideally, part of a medium-sized firms' international expansion. Those markets requiring large resources will not be possible initially, but with clever prioritizing of a potential expansion (from most promising to least promising markets) medium-sized firms can generate enough resources to start deepening their local presence.

CHAPTER 8

STRATEGIC AND BUSINESS ECONOMIC OUTLOOKS BY REGION[3]

The only function of economic forecasting is to make astrology look respectable.

— *J.K. Galbraith*

IN THIS OVERVIEW I provide a short analysis of strategic economic outlooks for emerging regions and some key markets. (This is just an executive summary and for more insights into different markets please get in touch with the author.)

EMERGING ASIA

"It is booming but we had that before. They were all Tiger economies in the 1990s and then all ended up in tears except China. I fear another boom and bust like we had in 1997." These are the words of a senior executive who was in Asia in the 1990s. Many companies lost huge amounts of money following the 1997 crisis, and needless to say some executives are still skeptical about the sustainability of growth in the region.

But emerging Asia in the late 1990s and today are very different places. If there was an outflow of short-term capital today (which largely caused the 1997 crisis), most emerging Asian countries

[3] This overview is an executive summary; for more information or for a more detailed presentation about emerging market economies please contact the author (nenad.pacek@globalsuccessadvisors.eu).

would have enough reserves to defend their currencies if they wanted to and would not have to go "cap in hand" to the IMF seeking bailout money (which always comes with strings attached, such as huge austerity programs that kill growth and business for a while).

Ever since the 1997 collapse, most economies in emerging Asia have made incredible improvements to their economic fundamentals (public debt, foreign debt, levels of foreign exchange reserves, budgets, current accounts), competitiveness, and quality of products, as well as beefing up their export engines. Many have something good to sell to the world. Some call it export dependency but as long as exports are diversified and can find global markets, it is a good dependency to have. Going forward, all Asian economies will have to spend more domestically and this is happening, but gradually. The fact that emerging Asia will continue to increase domestic spending in the next decade and beyond is wonderful news for long-term corporate planning and growth initiatives. Let's examine how emerging Asia improved its fundamentals.

- First, emerging Asia has a very low foreign debt accumulation. The weighted average of key markets shows just 17% of regional GDP (countries usually need external help when it hits 70% of GDP). This is the lowest regional foreign debt accumulation in the world.
- Second, public debt (which is such a burden today in the United States, Eurozone and Japan) is just 33% of regional GDP (about one third of average Eurozone or US public debt). Anything below 60% of GDP is considered sustainable. The important thing about these figures is that

they show emerging Asia will not need to deleverage in times of economic crisis. Without that need, it will be able to reach its growth potential and continually increase its purchasing power.
- Third, foreign exchange reserves are coming close to US $6 trillion, the largest accumulation of reserves of any region of the world (this figure excludes Japan and some small markets like Sri Lanka or Bhutan). In fact, Asia now holds some 70% of all foreign exchange reserves held by emerging economies. These reserves will continue to rise as governments continue to buy foreign exchange in a desire to keep their currencies relatively cheap and supportive of their export strategies.
- Fourth, the region runs a current account surplus, a rare thing these days anywhere in the world. In fact, all the larger Asian markets run a surplus, except India. This shows an underlying currency stability, and most likely a future currency appreciation trend. In fact, in the next 5–10 years, all emerging Asian economies will most likely see their currencies appreciate in both nominal and real terms. But Asian governments will also intervene against excessive appreciation. A word of caution is in order here, too. Later in this chapter I write about "hot money" inflows and outflows, and this could affect Asian currencies in the short term in unpredictable ways; but the key thing to remember is that countries can choose to defend their currencies with strong reserves. They did not have that option back in 1997–98.
- Fifth, the regional budget deficit is low at some 2% of GDP, and only in India, Malaysia and Vietnam it is higher when compared to international benchmarks.

RESILIENCE IN ASIAN MARKETS

Emerging Asia is currently the fastest growing region in the world both in terms of economic growth and for many firms also for their corporate sales. This is likely going to continue for the next 5–10 years, and possibly beyond. The region's resilience during the crisis was remarkable. When most world economies were collapsing in 2009, emerging Asia grew by more than 5%. Growth exploded to almost 9% in 2010, beating all other regions with ease. In the next five years, emerging Asia will grow some 7%, outperforming all other emerging markets, let alone the developed world. Sure, China's growth is not sustainable at these levels but politically it will be impossible to let growth rates sink below employment creation levels. The good news about growth in emerging Asia is that it is broad based and supported by exports, rising domestic demand but also (unlike in the developed world) by solid increases in domestic credit.

Most governments reacted well to the crisis in 2009 by introducing strong fiscal stimulus packages, deep cuts in interest rates and employment guarantees. As private and corporate confidence around the world and in the region went down in 2009, most governments in emerging Asia, unlike the developed world, will not need to deleverage.

Executives running global and regional operations should continue to be bullish about economic and business prospects in the region. Currencies will continue to appreciate and gradually an expanding proportion of economic growth will be generated by increases in domestic demand (household, corporate and government). It is a myth that emerging Asian consumers are not spending more than before. In the last six years, retail spending grew by more than 60%, and it is likely that this will continue for years to come.

Strategically, it makes perfect sense for companies to treat emerging Asia as the biggest priority for new business development investment and to explore more deeply all sales and manufacturing opportunities. China and India will continue to drive regional growth, but companies should not ignore other markets. Countries such as Indonesia and Malaysia will continue to do well. Executives should watch the twin deficits and some unsustainable policies in Vietnam, observe that Indian public debt does not go any higher from relatively high levels, make sure they understand that the savings rate in Korea is low, and appreciate the political risks in Thailand. But overall, these risks are relatively small and seen as manageable by seasoned executives, and do not ruin the broadly positive outlook for the region.

CHINA

China will continue to do well on the back of rising domestic spending (retail sales are currently up 14% year on year) as well as continued export orientation around undervalued renminbi and proactive economic management (in the case of a downturn, there will surely be another round of monetary and fiscal stimulus). I do not believe that China will allow fast appreciation of the renminbi in the foreseeable future (it might even push it down temporarily to keep the export engine growing as we enter a weak 2012 for world markets). Export growth is too important for job creation. The best executives can hope for regarding the value of the renminbi is to see up to a 5% annual appreciation against major world currencies. This will help sales in the years to come. It is hard to imagine the authorities allowing growth to fall below 8% a year, at least in the next five years. Everything under 8% does not generate enough jobs and undermines the regime's power.

China should be one of the biggest corporate priorities for years to come. We know that one day there will be political change in China and we also know that it might be a messy process. This is the risk for companies that keep investing in physical assets on the ground. But at the same time, this risk is incredibly difficult to quantify. The democratization of China might erupt next week, or in 20 years, or in 50 years. And because it is so difficult to predict, companies should simply keep selling and take calculated risks when it comes to investment in physical assets.

INDIA

India's outlook is probably less certain because of incoherent economic policies, rising corruption, frequent political paralysis and government about-faces that impact business and economic growth. However, the sheer size of the market simply dictates that every serious company must figure out how to grow there and outperform the competition on a sustainable basis. Despite the relatively uncertain outlook, it is important to remember that it would be highly surprising if India grows by less than 6% per year during the next decade. And of course the upside to this scenario is good.

To conclude, larger countries in emerging Asia ought to be economic winners over the next decade, with the possible exception of Vietnam, whose relatively high twin deficits (if not managed quickly) could push the country into temporary economic turmoil.

LATIN AMERICA

When I mention Latin America as a future business opportunity to about-to-retire global senior executives, the usual reaction is one of skepticism. "We lost our shirts a few times there and I would never invest much. It will never be sustainable," said one executive to me recently. If there is a continent that has a history of debt default and serious economic problems, Latin America was for years a symbol of that in international business circles.

But history is one thing and today's reality is another. The economic, political and business transformation of the last decade has been remarkable in a number of important countries. In 2010, Latin America was the second fastest growing area in the world in terms of economic growth and corporate sales. In 2011 it continued to do well for companies despite some slowdown in GDP growth, thanks largely to the unresolved European debt crisis. The most important development is that this growth is now underpinned by vastly improved economic fundamentals (foreign debt, public debt, foreign exchange reserves, current account, budget position). In fact, Latin America is now standing on stronger economic fundamentals than at any time in living memory. This is good news for future business. Let's look at those fundamentals.

- First, Latin America is not overly indebted anymore and debt was its Achilles' heel in the past. The continent's foreign debt is now among the lowest in the world, with a regional weighted average of key markets of just 20% of GDP

(economic history tells us that countries usually start to default or run into problems when their foreign debt reaches 70% of GDP).
- Second, public debt is just 45% of regional GDP, less than half of the levels in the Eurozone or the United States. At least on this criteria, most Latin American economies would qualify to join the Eurozone – unlike most Eurozone members, which do not.
- Third, foreign exchange reserves have gone up more than three times in the last 10 years and now exceed US $600 billion in key markets. In the likelihood of any economic turbulence, most governments have enough reserves to intervene in the currency markets. They can use central bank profits to help plug any deficits or make long-term investments in infrastructure spending and education.
- Fourth, the regional current account deficit is remarkably low at just 1.5% of regional GDP. Usually, currency pressures start when the current account deficit is about 4% of GDP or higher. Together with strong inflows of foreign direct investment this shows underlying currency stability. If anything, the risk for companies is too many inflows into some Latin American currencies (such as the Brazilian real) by speculators, which authorities will want to manage more in the future. This could cause some more depreciations in the future since some currencies are perhaps overbought at the time of writing.
- Fifth, the budget deficit is low as a regional aggregate (unlike in the EU, UK or the US), at around 2.5% of GDP.
- Sixth, interest rates are still hovering around an all time low and so helping improve access to finance for private

households and companies. And they will keep falling in the future (not in a straight line, though).

POLITICAL CHANGE

Behind this improvement in fundamentals has been a remarkable political transformation. Several years ago I was chairing a large business conference in Santiago with President Michelle Bachelet and the government of Chile. Having chaired over a hundred events of that kind around the world, I could not help but be impressed with the quality of government. And the most striking thing for me was a lack of ideological rigidity of any kind, a thing we all need so much of these days. When I remarked in one session that I couldn't place this government into any economic category, this response came from one of the top ministers:

> "We actually do not care if an idea comes from the right or the left. If we think an idea is good for the economic development of the country, for improving competitiveness or for reducing inequality to sustainable levels, we will embrace it and implement it regardless of its ideological origin."

This is striking to hear anywhere, and even more striking on a continent that was for many decades a playground of the Cold War powers, where countries lived in either leftist or rightist extremes. Today, there is more policy pragmatism, regardless of whether it is from a centre-left government in Brazil or a centre-right government in Colombia. Yes, we still have a few extremes, but their sustainability is questionable, and the number of such countries on the continent is shrinking. Brazil is a wonderful example of economic pragmatism. While the government still pushes an agenda of economic growth, reduction of social inequality and bigger social programs, at the same time it is not doing anything significant to damage the relationship with financial markets (on which it still partly depends for financing). It is a balancing act that Brazil has played so well under former president Lula.

The ongoing political transformation leads to more sustainable economic policies, a remarkable improvement in fundamentals, an unprecedented rise of domestic firms, and an unprecedented increase in foreign direct investment interest, while a commitment to reducing inequality will also improve growth sustainability and opportunities for companies in the coming years.

Strategically, companies should put Latin America on the list of areas that now deserve ever growing investment and a deeper local presence.

SUSTAINED GROWTH

Growth was resilient during the global crisis when GDP fell just 1.8%. The 2010 bounce back was remarkable and growth reached just over 6%. Regional growth is likely to continue at 4.5–5% until 2020 (with a somewhat sharper slowdown in 2012 as the world economy slows). Most currencies are likely to experience further appreciation pressures over time and some will continue to be targets of speculative portfolio investments (this means short term volatility in some currencies is a possibility). After the IMF stated that capital controls on short-term capital movements are not a bad idea after all, we can expect more measures by governments in the region to stop speculative inflows that can push currencies to levels that are out of line with fundamentals, followed by sharp falls as speculative money suddenly leaves (see below the short discussion on economic risks in emerging markets).

However, the risks going forward are still many. Part of the region's growth is still driven by commodities. A flow of money out of commodity markets would shave off some growth in Latin America, and this surely will happen from time to time since commodity markets are schizophrenic.

The second risk, which is more medium term, arises from the following questions: will Latin American economies manage to diversify their economies, will they manage to consistently reduce inequality, reduce crime and improve access to education at all levels? Speed in these issues matters. If people see that there is economic stability, but they make no personal gain from it, the risk arises that some countries could slip back into more ideological forms of economic management.

The third risk is that Latin America is still a popular playground for portfolio investment, some of which is purely speculative in nature. If currencies get too strong on the back of such speculative inflows, this would increase current account deficits, foreign debt will begin to rise and local exports would start to die. Cynically, this would be a good short-term period for foreign companies, since stronger currencies would reduce import prices and make people feel a bit richer. But imbalances would grow and trouble would be stored for later.

Countries that are likely to have good sustainable growth in the near future are Brazil, Chile and Colombia. Mexico continues to be dependent on US growth and this could mean that it might not be able to grow more than 3.5% in the next few years. Argentina is booming, but this is partly driven by a commodity boom and partly by a few unsustainable economic policies. Peru is doing well but this is mainly down to a commodity-driven boom. Panama will continue to grow some 7% in the next few years. Venezuela, Ecuador and Bolivia will be relative laggards. The good news is that the big markets are likely to do well for years to come.

CENTRAL AND EASTERN EUROPE

I call my clients who run Central and Eastern Europe "CEOs", or "Chief Explaining Officers". They enjoyed a boom from 1999–2008, but now it is a struggle in many markets. But it is hard to explain that to global headquarters.

In 2011 and 2012, the CEE region underperformed other emerging regions for the third and forth years in a row. Companies there will not be able to rely much on external economic conditions to drive sales growth for a few years. How things change. Between 1999 and mid-2008, CEE outperformed all emerging regions and enjoyed an unprecedented decade of fast growth, appreciating currencies and general optimism. During that time there were only sporadic slowdowns in a few countries, but on aggregate the region performed strongly. Sales jumped year on year and new investments were channeled into the region. Foreign direct investment reached an unprecedented US $140 billion in 2007 – more than China and India combined.

But as the global crisis hit, it turned out that a number of growth drivers were not sustainable. Underlying weaknesses were suddenly exposed: 2009 was a disastrous year for virtually all multinational companies, and 2010 and 2011 proved to be challenging years for business in most sectors and the majority of countries. The problem is that most of GDP growth in CEE is currently driven by exports, rather than domestic demand. And domestic demand will be slow to improve until at least 2014.

When the global financial system imploded, the CEE region was among the first to feel the consequences, because of its large dependency on external financing and large exposure to loans. On top of that, it also did not react well to the crisis.

Regional GDP declined by 5.9% in 2009, after growing 5.9% per year on average between 2000 and 2008. The best years were 2006 and 2007, when growth exceeded 7%, fuelling record corporate sales and profit growth. An unsustainable credit bubble means that 7% plus growth will not be reached again for decades.

Today, most of the region's recovery is driven by exports and high commodity prices (the latter helping the likes of Russia and Kazakhstan, for example). Domestic demand is extremely weak and will stay weak for a few more years in high foreign debt markets, such as Hungary, Slovenia, Croatia, Estonia and Latvia; relatively high foreign debt markets include the likes of Serbia, Ukraine, Lithuania, Slovakia, Bulgaria and Romania. These markets will be going through deleveraging at both a household and a corporate level, and this will hurt economic growth and business in the next few years.

The CIS markets are fundamentally much better, especially Russia, Kazakhstan and Azerbaijan. But with their currently high growth is largely linked to high commodity prices. Poland and the Czech Republic have acceptable fundamentals. Poland is still doing OK thanks to pro-growth government policies (although a new round of austerity will slow things there temporarily, too) but Czech Republic has stopped growing thanks to a tough austerity program and slowing exports to the EU.

There are several reasons why the regional recovery has been weak when it comes to domestic demand (with notable exceptions in the biggest CIS markets and Poland):

1. On aggregate, the region has more foreign debt than other emerging regions. This means it has started the process of deleveraging and many markets are also embracing austerity. Any country that goes through deleveraging of household, corporate and government debt always does so at the expense of growth and purchasing power. That has always been the case in economic history and it will be this time.
2. Credit collapsed and now is slow to return – in fact credit flows are still falling in highly-leveraged markets. Most banks are foreign-owned, so they need to deleverage and beef up their balance sheets at mother banks level. This is happening at the expense of lending growth.

3. Overall, the governments' reaction when the crisis began was inferior to other emerging regions (i.e., no monetary stimulus; no employment guarantees; and embracing austerity measures when corporate and private confidence was low).
4. As unemployment rose, household confidence collapsed, pushing household spending down – in some markets even into double digits. Overall private confidence is still low in highly leveraged markets, and without a vigorous recovery in private spending there can be no GDP growth.
5. Many markets – such as Hungary, Romania, Latvia, Serbia and Ukraine – needed IMF (and/or EU) emergency money to prevent outright default and bankruptcies. And the IMF money comes with strings attached for most countries (except good pupils like Poland, who can draw funds from the newly created Flexible Credit Line without any conditions). The strings are known: cut spending and keep interest rates high – an approach that is opposite to what other markets were doing to get out of the slump in confidence.
6. The Western Europe outlook in terms of domestic demand for CEE exports is weak as the Eurozone struggles with its public debt crisis.

VARIABLE GROWTH

Growth will be uneven across the region over the next few years. It will be weaker in markets with high foreign debt and in need of deleveraging. But it will be stronger in less leveraged markets. Less leveraged markets include Russia, Turkey, Poland, Czech Republic – the first two in particular should be excellent for business for years to come (unless oil price falls and kills parts of business in Russia). All four have good fundamentals but Russia has virtually no public debt, its foreign debt is low and it is sitting on the fourth largest accumulation of foreign exchange reserves in the world.

Business is growing well in Russia but oil prices do constitute a risk. If prices were to fall to under US $60 per barrel or even threaten to go in that direction, the rouble would experience pressures and businesses will be hit. Political instability could create risks in the future, although most companies now choose to ignore this threat since it is difficult to quantify (like in China).

Turkey will be one of the most exciting emerging markets in the world in the coming years, despite the current slowdown caused by economic overheating and some recent pressures on the Turkish lira. The fundamentals are broadly good and the good news is that the government is trying to manage the reliance on short-term financing from abroad better than it has in the past. To reduce its large current account deficit, I think the Turkish government will continue to favour a weaker lira rather than having to rely on external borrowing. This will hurt sales and business in the short term, but it is good news for future sustainability, and over the medium term it will good for business.

Poland and the Czech Republic sit on good fundamentals and will do reasonably well in the future, although short-term business prospects are being hurt by austerity programs and by some speculative outflows that have hurt both currencies (especially the

Polish zloty). Further east, commodity-driven Kazakhstan and Azerbaijan will do well as long as prices are good; but these are not necessarily competitive economies once one removes from the equation the commodity variable.

FUTURE PROSPECTS

With sales weak throughout CEE, many developed world companies are somehow losing CEE from their radar screens. This kind of outlook is too short-termist. I am deeply convinced that CEE is not a second-rate emerging market. Why?

These days it is easy for multinational headquarters to jump to the conclusion that CEE can be largely ignored as a priority sales/business development destination (except Russia and Turkey). Regional sales and profit growth is significantly weaker than in emerging Asia, and weaker than Latin America, MENA and even Sub-Saharan Africa. This is in sharp contrast to CEE being the best in the world for corporate sales growth between 1999 and mid-2008.

At several of our recent CEEMEA Business Group regional directors meetings, we have heard comments that regional directors were increasingly struggling to get resources for the CEE, that most attention was on other regions and that stretch budgets for 2012 were still too ambitious for what the region can offer over the next two years. I would strongly argue that once deleveraging in many CEE markets is over and we come to the end of 2014, the CEE region will again be a very exciting place in terms of sales growth. The current crisis is temporary and partly cyclical. The region has many fundamental strengths, which means that CEE has a solid, sustainable future ahead. These strengths are:

- CEE economies are significantly more diversified than those in Latin America, the Middle East or Africa, and are not dependent on one or two strong commodities
- Education levels are high, which feeds competitiveness
- These economies usually combine stable social structures and low taxation
- There is a solid SME sector in many markets
- The region has happy foreign investors (who invested in manufacturing for exports) which will keep returning
- Public debt is relatively low and much better than Western Europe
- Highly indebted markets are swallowing the hard medicine now and they will come out of the crisis with vastly improved balance sheets at private, corporate and government levels
- Traditional drivers of growth are gradually returning, and this will gently accelerate over the next two years
- Not all markets are highly indebted and the likes of Russia, Turkey and Poland offer solid growth opportunities, even in the short term.

MIDDLE EAST AND NORTH AFRICA (MENA)

Between 2003 and 2008 the MENA region grew on average by 5.7%. With regional growth at 1.4% in 2009, the region was resilient compared to other regions of the world (the only more resilient region was emerging Asia), but still exceptionally challenging, as many key markets sharply deteriorated.

MENA recovered in 2010 and grew by an estimated 4.1%. But social and political unrest are threatening the outlook for at least several markets. Arab Spring reduced growth to under 4% in 2011. If Egypt and Tunisia achieve some form of normality soon, regional growth will easily reach 4.5% in the next few years – which will be similar to Latin America, a bit worse than Asia and Sub-Saharan Africa, but much better than Central and Eastern Europe (which is still deleveraging after the economic crisis). High oil prices are currently helping major oil exporters and those economies are booming. This is especially the case after the "Arab Spring" revolutions boosted oil prices.

IMPACT OF OIL PRICES ON CORPORATE APPROACHES

From an economic perspective, the MENA region has often lacked underlying sustainability during the last 15–20 years. And it is not surprising that this underlying problem has dictated how companies have treated the MENA region. These uncertainties spilled over into corporate perceptions and many regional directors have therefore struggled to get more resources to build a sustainable business in the region. When oil prices were low (between 1985 and 2004 they were US $9–$30 per barrel – and mostly around $20), many companies simply treated the region as an opportunistic cash cow, employing a corporate structure largely relying on remote partners and a strategy that was too regional. Most companies did not put enough resources on the ground, especially at country level.

When oil prices started to climb rapidly from 2004 (culminating at US $147 per barrel in July 2008), corporate results in hydrocarbon exporting nations improved beyond recognition. The results were also boosted in several previously sleepy markets in North Africa as their economies started improving. Simultaneously, Lebanon continued to defy gravity despite massive debts, and Dubai was riding a debt wave. No wonder companies started to think how to further improve on newly strong results in MENA and more importantly, how to institutionalize sales growth into lasting success that would outperform the competition over an extended period of time. In other words, corporate strategies started to shift from opportunistic remoteness to systematic depth.

RECENT CORPORATE INVESTMENT

The period from 2005 until today has been exceptionally active in terms of systematic corporate investment in business development, brand-building and local presence. In a few years prior to 2011 Arab Spring, corporate desire to do more in MENA increased to all-time highs, especially in hydrocarbon driven economies but also in Egypt, Tunisia or Algeria. On the back of stronger economic fundamentals, the competition was heating up in MENA (just like in other strongly performing regions), pushing more companies to become more serious about the region.

But just as companies had started to treat the MENA region more seriously and many plans have been put in place to invest more in business development, the political risks (which was latent and hard to quantify for years) suddenly increased, with instability first in Tunisia and Egypt, and then in Libya, Syria and tiny Bahrain. These eruptions have caused companies to wonder if similar events might occur in Saudi Arabia, Kuwait, Algeria, Jordan and Morocco. The elevated political uncertainty will linger on, and global perceptions about the region will probably cause many companies to put major investments on hold, at least in riskier markets. However, companies should continue to invest in strong oil exporting nations to build faster sales growth. These markets are fundamentally good in terms of debt levels and reserves and are booming on the back of high oil prices.

STRONG FUNDAMENTALS

MENA economic fundamentals are some of the best in the world. Total official and unofficial reserves, plus the amounts accumulated in sovereign wealth funds, probably exceed US $2.5 trillion dollars. This is the second largest regional accumulation of reserves after emerging Asia. The reserves accumulation is also higher than emerging Asia on a per capita basis and also as a percentage of regional GDP. Even if oil prices fall, the reserves could keep spending going for several years in a number of oil exporting markets (which are in any case most promising for business in the next few years).

Total government debt as a percentage of GDP is low, particularly in oil exporting markets. Oil exporting markets have an aggregate government debt of 18% of GDP. This is one of the lowest percentages in the world. The only markets with government debt exceeding 60% of GDP (the international benchmark of sustainability) in MENA are Lebanon (over 130%), Egypt (over 85%, and rising after further unrest) and Jordan (64%). Only Lebanon is worse off than Western Europe, but it keeps defying gravity!

The external debt burden in MENA is small, too, at just 27% of regional GDP. When countries do not have a need for deleveraging they also grow better or closer to their potential. The only markets in MENA where external debt is higher than it should be (i.e., 70% of GDP) are Lebanon (155%), Bahrain (140%), Qatar (70% – but not worrying considering strong exports and sizeable reserves) and Dubai (if we treat it as a separate entity), where external debt is estimated at 115% of GDP. In these places, growth will be below potential for a few years.

The above debt accumulations are important for future growth – unlike the developed world, most MENA markets do not need to deleverage, which should help them reach their growth potential, especially if oil prices remain robust. With strong oil prices, the region is running a current account surplus, with the exceptions of Iraq, Yemen, Jordan, Lebanon and Morocco (where the current account deficits are higher than they should be, therefore indicating some potential currency pressures).

DANGERS AND RISKS

MENA accounts for some 3% of global GDP (at market exchange rates). For a typical, well-established multinational, MENA accounts for about 3% of global revenues. Regional growth is highly dependent on public spending, and the size of public spending is often dependent on commodity prices. If commodity prices fall, so will the scale of public spending. Public announcements about major spending packages are sometimes not fully implemented and just serve a PR purpose. Therefore, it is dangerous to predicate a business plan on that alone. Bank lending will stay subdued. Banks are more cautious due to the new Basel III rules. Also, many foreign banks have had their fingers burned, particularly in the Gulf in the aftermath of the Dubai debt crisis, and are more cautious.

The biggest risks for MENA are oil prices and political instability. The best thing that companies can do is to keep focusing on developing sales by building a stronger local presence. Of course, when it comes to decisions about building factories, companies must be more careful, taking into account local conditions.

OUTLOOK

The economic winners for business in the next few years will be Saudi Arabia, Abu Dhabi (as the wealthiest of the United Arab Emirates), Qatar, Oman and, if political paralysis allows enough spending, Kuwait. Israel will, as usual, behave more in line with the business cycle in its key export markets, which are mostly in developed nations. Therefore growth will be a bit softer in the short term but good over the medium term, provided political issues do not explode one way or the other.

Iraq should boom on the back of rising oil output, provided that security can be managed after US troops pull out. Iran, potentially one of the most exciting markets in the world due to its size, will struggle under yet another round of sanctions, and down the road also a potential military strike. Morocco and Algeria will continue to provide steady growth in the future, provided that hydrocarbon prices stay attractive for Algeria and if both countries avoid political turmoil.

Egypt is currently a political and economic mess, without clarity on how the revolution will finish, but the country is unlikely to have an effective technocratic government of the type it had prior to the crisis (and which was so good for business). Tunisia should be a good market provided that real elections in 2012 offer some political stability. Libya will restore its pre-war oil output by late 2012 or early 2013. If local political and tribal factions can agree on future policy, Libya should be an exciting emerging market for years to come (although its small population size will limit corporate activities). Lebanon will continue to struggle under high debts and significantly elevated political risks. Most companies expect the steady, unexciting business environment in Jordan to continue.

SUB-SAHARAN AFRICA

Sub-Saharan Africa is attracting the attention of companies wishing to expand business to new territories. Sales growth is solid in many markets and there is less competition (although it is rising, particularly from Chinese companies). However, in absolute terms, sales are low.

The economic outlook is not bad as long as commodity prices stay reasonably high. The region had several very good years in terms of growth in the pre-crisis period. Between 2003 and 2008, the region grew by 6.2%, or twice as fast as the 1990–2002 average. The rise in commodity prices, inflows of FDI, stronger currencies, debt write-offs, donor inflows, the rise of South Africa and Nigeria, and improvements in fundamentals all contributed to a strong pre-crisis performance.

But the region was not immune to the global crisis. In 2009, regional growth was just 2.1%, and in per capita terms the region was barely growing. But compared to other regions, Sub-Saharan Africa was quite resilient, largely (and sadly) due to a lack of integration with the global economy. Credit was flat (unlike in developed regions), donor money kept coming in and this helped resilience.

The relatively good news is that the region is now recovering well on the back of:
- higher commodity prices
- ongoing donor inflows
- a gradual recovery in South Africa (which could be better)
- strong growth in Nigeria (despite political issues)
- generally good central banks' reactions to the crisis (i.e., looser monetary policies)
- gently improving credit conditions
- stronger economic fundamentals
- improved reserves due to the IMF's allocation of SDRs (which helped stability and enabled some public spending increases)
- recovery in overseas workers' remittances
- rising IMF lending
- rising FDI and financing from China
- some improvement in corporate spending (largely drawn from corporate reserves)
- higher public spending in most markets (70% of the countries managed to actually increase public spending).

All of the above resulted in stronger domestic demand. Growth should easily exceed 5% in the foreseeable future. This is respectable compared to other regions of the world during the post-crisis period. But Sub-Saharan Africa would have to grow by at least 8% for a long period to really start improving living standards. A mere 5–6% growth is simply not enough to make a significant difference.

RISKS

The three principal risks to potential growth are lower commodity prices, lower donor inflows and higher food prices. Donor inflows could become more erratic as developed markets struggle with their own record public debt burdens (there are already preliminary signs that donor money might be slowing in the next two to three years). Executives should also be aware that headline GDP figures can be heavily driven by exports of commodities and that domestic demand tends to be weaker than headline figures.

- Sub Saharan Africa accounts for just over 1% of global GDP (at market exchange rates).
- For a typical, well-established multinational, Sub-Saharan Africa accounts for just over 1% of their global revenues.
- While the region offers good growth opportunities, its absolute size in the global economy is small – hardly enough to fully compensate for any weak business in the developed world.

The biggest market in terms of GDP, South Africa, is not growing well and is now re-examining its economic priorities regarding growth, employment and cheaper exchange rates. However, Nigeria is growing well and companies are increasingly prioritizing this large market of some 150 million people.

Other markets attracting corporate attention now are Angola (oil), Zambia (copper), Ghana (also oil driven), Ethiopia (with some 80 million people) and Kenya (services driven, no big commodities to export). Other markets also worth considering are Mozambique, Tanzania, Uganda, Senegal, Cameroon and the Democratic Republic of Congo, Botswana and Namibia.

It is key to note that competition is not as fierce as in other emerging regions and that one can carve out good, profitable positions and fast growth in many markets. Companies should note, though, a tremendous increase in competition from China and India, as well as from major multinationals that are designing new Africa strategies as we speak.

CHAPTER 9

SELECTED ECONOMIC RISKS EXECUTIVES SHOULD BE AWARE OF

The freeing of financial markets to pursue their casino instincts heightens the odds of crises… Because unlike a casino, the financial markets are inextricably linked with the world outside, the real economy pays the price.

—*Lawrence Summers*

BELOW ARE THE MAIN RISK factors you should monitor and be aware of when investing and building business in emerging economies.

HOT MONEY IMPACT ON CURRENCIES

Not all aspects of globalization are positive. Premature opening of capital flows, especially short-term capital flows, has continued to create huge problems for economies around the world. The fact that you and I can buy any currency, T-bill or government bond that we like might sound like a good idea from a selfish point of view (why should I not be able to put my savings into Hungarian government bonds and earn 9%?; what do I care if a market is run so badly that it always has to borrow?). But this premature increase of short-term flows has created more difficulties for economies than almost any other issue over the last couple of decades (especially in developing economies). We can link most emerging markets crises (Mexico 1994, Asia 1997, Russia 1998, Brazil 1999) in some shape or form to the premature liberalization of the capital account.

Now imagine some large investment funds want to make a 7% return in South Africa (yes, they actually do!). And many keep buying South African rand and government debt securities to achieve their short term yield goals. Buyers do well as long as there is no panic sell off. What does that kind of foreign "hot money" inflow do to the recipient economy?

First, it could push the currency to appreciate beyond its trade and foreign direct investment fundamentals. This would make imports cheaper and make people there feel richer. They would buy more imported goods. The banks would feel good and would lend to a richer population. Banks would borrow from abroad short-term and give out long-term loans, creating a dangerous mismatch in case of a reversal of fortunes. But exports would suffer. The resulting current account deficit would increase foreign debt. If this goes on too long, the recipient country would probably end up with a high foreign debt and the need to deleverage. And any deleveraging always comes at the expense of growth and purchasing power. Business would suffer.

But the bigger problem for business is when those who put their money into South Africa looking for high short-term yields suddenly decide to withdraw it for even higher returns elsewhere. And imagine it happens as a panic sell off, like it did in Asia in 1997. Everybody wants to suddenly off-load that government bond or T-bill (denominated in local currency) and no one wants to take any losses. The sudden outflow of "hot money" always hurts economies very quickly and, as we saw in Asia in 1997 or in September–October 2011 in many emerging economies, it can lead to rapid currency depreciations (even in well-managed countries) and can almost overnight bring catastrophe for affected economy and for all businesses operating in them.

"Hot money" sudden and fast outflows can lead to a currency crisis, continues with banks calling in loans (both foreign and domestic banks), investment and consumer confidence collapses, GDP falls, corporate sales decline. (For a more detailed account of how "hot money" influenced several emerging market crises in the 1990s, please refer to my earlier book, *Emerging Markets*).

Ideological causes

If "hot money" inflows and sudden outflows can cause so many problems for economies and businesses, then we have to ask: who pushed the idea, why are they still around and are future crises possible? The light regulation and liberalization doctrine that started to dominate global economic thinking several decades ago was the fertile source for pushing capital account liberalization onto countries that were not ready for it (see the feature on "Partial Failure of Economics" in my new executive handbook, *Global Economy*).

So partly the push for capital account liberalization was ideological. It was forgotten that Western European countries, for example, did not fully liberalize controls on capital account movements (particularly on the short-term ones that cause most difficulties) for up to five decades after the end of World War II. Most of them liberalized gradually after reaching a certain level of wealth, stability and global competitiveness. In other words, they were able to develop without facing the risk that speculative capital inflows and outflows carry for the real economy.

But ideology is not the whole story. Jagdish Bagwhati from Columbia University argued in his excellent book, *In Defense of Globalization*, that it was the "power elite" of Wall Street, the US Treasury and the IMF, plus the "energetic lobbying" of financial firms, which pushed the liberalization of capital accounts on countries that were not ready. They saw their business interests as pushing for unlimited movement of capital around the world.

Sadly, the doctrine is still around and "hot money" inflows and outflows are an ongoing threat to the health of many exposed economies, even those that are reasonably well managed and that have good economic fundamentals. The only thing that has changed is that many emerging economies have learned the lessons of recent crises and have beefed up their foreign exchange reserves, which serve as a buffer against sudden outflows. Many also corrected their economic fundamentals by reducing the size of their public and foreign debts (see my earlier regional analysis).

However, for businesses operating in the international arena, the risk of sudden excessive appreciation of currencies and then sudden depreciation is still here. Companies and executives need to pay ongoing attention to this by examining the economic fundamentals of the countries in which they operate: assess the size of "hot money" parked in the country; assess the worst-case scenario in case of outflows; and most importantly, by communicating the risks upward to the headquarters to manage expectations (and to protect careers). The last thing an executive wants is to be blamed for weak results caused by unexpected depreciation.

Controlling hot money

Recently we have seen several countries, like Brazil, imposing taxes on "hot money" inflows, in an attempt to discourage them. This is the right thing to do. Those who argue that such taxes reduce foreign direct investment are either wrong or have a vested interest in saying so. There is enough scientific evidence to show that excessive "hot money" inflows and outflows hurt economies and business, and no country should be a hostage to the narrow interests of a few bankers and economic ideologues.

There is one significant thing that countries can do, too. They can borrow more domestically and can run sustainable economic policies with low deficits and debts (thereby reducing the need for external borrowing). They can also have their central banks buy government debt during economic downturns, since this typically does not cause the inflation rate to rise. We also have to remember that countries like China that had capital controls did not experience the Asian crisis of 1997–98. (They asked those who wanted to buy their currency: "Why do you need it? For yield? You are not going to build a factory? Go home then!") The same was true for Chile and Slovenia during similar episodes.

What are the chances that at least some capital controls will become entrenched as a normal part of economic policy of all countries? A few months ago my answer would have been, "Very slim". But now, with the latest endorsement of the IMF for more capital controls, the chances are better that common sense will prevail. I wouldn't bet too much of my money on full implementation, but the latest news gives us some limited encouragement.

What are the implications for business? If capital controls are more widely used, currencies will not appreciate beyond their fundamentals, the risk of sudden depreciations and economic meltdowns would subside and business predictability and sustainability would be easier to achieve. Non-financial companies should lobby hard for more capital controls as a way to avoid massive volatility and sudden losses in markets around the world.

COMMODITY PRICES AS A RISK TO BUSINESS PLANNING

Commodity prices will continue to rise as populations grow. In 50 years' time there will probably be 2 billion extra people on our planet. Demographics will lead to more demand for commodities – there is little doubt about that. As the world gradually consumes more commodities, prices should also gradually rise. From time to time, panic over supply will cause prices to rise (political turmoil in the Middle East might cause oil price spikes temporarily, and a bad harvest or rough climate patches will do the same to food prices). On aggregate, commodity prices have more than doubled in recent years. But we have also had greater volatility with commodity prices than usual. And this recent high volatility is a threat to many commodity exporters (and businesses operating with them) and a threat to many firms that are struggling with ever more rapidly changing input prices.

But the bigger issue is the impact of highly volatile commodity prices on the macroeconomic stability of emerging nations and the impact on the purchasing power of many people around the world. Sharp short-term price spikes cause inflation rates to rise, putting central bankers in a difficult position. Should we increase interest rates because of this and kill a fragile economic recovery? Or should we allow the inflation rate to get out of (temporary) control for the sake of promoting growth? In the business world many executives will suffer as they build business plans but high commodity prices hurt their buyers and cause havoc with profit margins.

So why are commodity prices more volatile than usual? Many commodity prices have not behaved in line with fundamentals over the last five or six years. Prices jumped 50% just between March 2010 and March 2011. Has demand increased that much and has the supply really fallen that much during that period? Certainly not. Commodity prices have been a bit like a psychotic patient without drugs to calm him down.

I recall speaking about the world economy to a group of commodity traders just before the global crisis. During the break, one of them approached me. He was close to retirement and said: "I have been in this business for 35 years. The first 32 years were all similar. We knew what we were doing! And then I had to relearn everything again. Speculation and leveraged speculation are rampant.

Commodities are nothing but a huge casino." I remember his words every time I see how insane and sudden some commodity price movements are. And how much human, economic and business pain sudden high prices can cause.

Oil price variations

To illustrate the insanity, let's examine oil prices (oil is the craziest example). Here are a few facts about oil – you can draw your own conclusions about its sudden price movements.

1. Oil fundamentals have not changed much in the last 20 years. Yes, emerging economies are consuming more, but developed markets are consuming less. Oil demand/consumption has not exceeded 1.7% per year in the last decade (except for being a bit stronger during 2010's bounce back from 2009 lows) and yet the price has shot up from an average of US $20 per barrel in the early 1990s to $147 in 2008. It fell from US $147 to under $40 per barrel when the global crisis started in 2008, although the actual fall in oil consumption around the world was barely 3%. And then it went up from under US $40 to $120 in 2012 (after the Arab Spring and issues with Iran), but with oil consumption growth during 2010–2011 at some 2% annually. You can bet that this cannot be linked to simple issues of supply and demand.

2. There is adequate supply of oil until at least 2015. Stocks are high and just in the OPEC countries there is almost 6 million barrels per day of spare capacity (which is forecasted to shrink to 3.5m b/d spare capacity). This is historically a high surplus. Even if Iran explodes there is enough spare capacity in Saudi Arabia to compensate for any global shortfall.

3. Supply should steadily increase in the next few years, notably in Brazil and Iraq.
4. The world economic outlook, and therefore demand for oil, is not great for 2012–2015. In 2011 world growth was a modest 2.5% (at market exchange rates) as the developed world struggled with massive debts and deleveraging. Emerging markets also slowed down in 2011 from a strong 2010 bounce-back as fiscal and monetary stimulus packages were withdrawn in Asia and Latin America, and as they struggled to export to the developed world. There is simply no big boom in oil consumption on the horizon over the next few years. Unless there is demand on some other planet!
5. Over the last 50 years, OPEC has produced 400 billion barrels of oil, but still holds an incredible estimate of 1.2 trillion barrels in reserves. Some observers think this is a conservative estimate of remaining reserves.
6. The global search for alternative energies has gone beyond the tipping point. The developed world (where oil consumption is already falling) will steadily reduce its need for hydrocarbon products in the next 10–20 years and alternative technologies will begin to appear in emerging markets, too.
7. Some major oil producers say in private that the real oil price is anywhere between US $40 and $55 per barrel.
8. Some oil producers and commodity traders say that for every purchase of a real (physical) barrel of oil, there are currently four to five purchases of various forward contracts (just paper investments, where investors never actually see the underlying commodity). For gasoline it is even worse: for every physical barrel traded there are up to seven futures contracts. Why is

there such rampant speculation? Because it is allowed and because some of the major players are gambling with someone else's money. And it is probably allowed because it suits a few vested interests.

9. When the oil bubble reached its high in mid 2008 (at US $147 per barrel), some banks estimated that there was more than US $500 billion of speculative money in the oil market alone. Today, the extra liquidity from printing money (today popularly called "quantitative easing") and lack of good investments in developed markets has shifted massive amounts of short term "investments" into commodities, including oil. Luckily, speculators cannot make massive leveraged commodity bets (i.e., borrow to buy forward contracts) anymore, since the days of the global credit bubble are behind us, at least for the foreseeable future.

10. The inflow of cash into commodities continues. Various banks estimate that between US $50 and $80 billion of additional cash moved into commodities during 2011.

11. My private conversations with several commodity traders indicate that 40–50% of commodity markets today are controlled by those seeking nothing more than short-term yields and/or speculative profit.

12. Sadly, commodities have become just another form of financial investment. Over the last decade, the birth of commodity indices as well as the creation of the ETFs (exchange traded funds) have enabled just about anyone to "invest" in commodities. The US government reports that the value of global investment in commodities' so-called index funds has gone up from US $15 billion to $200 billion.

Today there are almost seven hundred exchange-traded products out there dealing with commodities that you and I can "invest" in.

13. It is time governments around the world worked on banning commodity trading based on short-term yields. But they are always behind the curve – recently, a top US regulator has said that sadly "…we will delay new caps that would curb big commodity bets". Long live the commodities casino!
14. The Dodd Frank reforms are trying to regulate OTC (over-the-counter) commodity derivatives, but no one is paying attention to unregulated physical commodities. The industry has again won the lobbying game.
15. Traders and banks are again finding a loophole in the physical commodities space. Believe it or not, there are more and more funds that actually buy physical commodities and keep them stored in newly-built warehouses. Of course, it doesn't matter that I will never actually need a barrel of oil or a few hundred kilos of copper. Now we can own commodities without actually having to open the usual requirement called a "futures trading account". And we can even go and see our purchase, owned by an investment bank, in a warehouse, perhaps somewhere close to New York.

As you can see, based on the fundamentals of supply and demand, oil should not really be trading at more than US $50–60 per barrel. It is interesting to see that some of the older Gulf oil exporters keep the oil price below US $60 in their government budgets. They know the real story.

IMPLICATIONS FOR BUSINESS

So what are the chances that governments around the world will work to eliminate speculative commodity trading, and particularly, various leveraged bets? I doubt much will be done any time soon. Some aspects of commodity trading have now become "normal", and many strange activities are not even being questioned by anyone.

What are the implications for business? The big issue for many companies is: do we pass the higher input prices to our customers and protect our margins, or do we play a more sensitive game with a sensitive post-crisis buyer and aim for increasing market share against those who decide to increase prices? This is a typical dilemma many executives have recently faced in many emerging economies.

A further destabilizing factor could be that many firms that need, for example, metal commodities will try to accumulate some reserves before prices rise further – and thereby cause a further increase in prices. Over time, many manufacturers will try to get their R&D departments to use new, innovative ways of manufacturing that use fewer raw materials. But in the short term, there is no easy way out and executives know that extreme price volatility is here to stay. If anything, high input prices will prompt even more companies to evaluate their manufacturing costs closely and then seek to move even more of the facilities to cheaper locations.

The big commodity-related risk for firms is that many countries in emerging markets are often dependent on just a few key commodities. Just scan the emerging market world of the Middle East, Africa, Latin America or parts of the former Soviet Union. If commodity prices fall sharply, many commodity exporters suffer in terms of possible depreciations, lack of government revenues and ultimately impact on business. The best executives can do is to write footnotes below their business plans, something along the lines of: "Mr CEO, we operate in Russia very well, but do not blame me if the price of oil falls, impacts the rouble, and then our business." Any company operating in commodity-driven markets must have more robust contingency plans than elsewhere.

OVERALL LEVEL OF PUBLIC AND FOREIGN DEBT

To assess growth potential in the upcoming period, executives should be aware of the level of public and foreign debt in emerging markets in which they operate, or wish to operate. These numbers are well tracked in most countries and easily available. They tell a lot to an executive who is about to put a three or five year plan together. The need to deleverage can be a powerful drag on growth and is a risk.

Both public and foreign debt should be as low as possible. Anything higher than 60% of GDP for public debt, and anything higher than 70% of GDP for foreign debt, usually means some deleveraging will be necessary. It is also important to track more immediate repayments of debt and the ability of countries to pay for upcoming obligations. Excessive public debt means that governments are likely to go through deleveraging: this is usually achieved by increasing taxes alongside cuts in public spending (and in rare cases by running large inflation rates or by defaulting on debts); in a few fortunate locations, this happens via strong pro-growth policies. Whatever the policy response to high public debt, executives should be aware of its size and warn their bosses of potential deleveraging. This is particularly important for businesses that are highly dependent on government spending to grow their sales in emerging markets, such as IT or healthcare companies.

In case of excessive corporate or household debts, there is also a need to deleverage. Companies should monitor the size, assess the likelihood of deleveraging and estimate the potential impact on domestic demand. Looking at past episodes of deleveraging because of high levels of foreign debt, they do tend to go on for a long time: in the best cases, the deleveraging sequence can be over in two to three years, but in the worst cases it can go on for eight to nine years. The longer such deleveraging lasts, the weaker sales growth will be.

LEVEL OF FOREIGN EXCHANGE RESERVES

Low levels of foreign exchange reserves used to be a major vulnerability of many emerging markets. Luckily, things have improved beyond recognition and emerging markets now hold over 75% of all global foreign exchange reserves. Still, executives should be aware of the forex levels in countries in which they operate. This indicates the ability of authorities to intervene and protect against any depreciation pressure. Lack of reserves or no sufficient reserves can indicate an inability to defend domestic currencies. The right level of forex reserves before the crisis was seen as the value of three months of imports, but most observers now point out that the safer level is around five months of imports. Keep checking this indicator: it is easily available on all central bank websites.

In addition to monitoring the forex level, executives should also assess whether the reserves are on a downward or upward trend, and explore any reasons why either might be the case. In the case of sharply falling reserves (as in Egypt in 2011–2012), it shows that a country is intervening to protect against depreciation and in case it runs out of reserves; this development could lead to a significant economic downturn, major depreciation and the creation of parallel foreign exchange markets.

CURRENT ACCOUNT BALANCE

The current account balance is a good risk indicator in terms of potential currency movements and the build-up of foreign debt. It is easy to monitor, although executives should be aware that the balance can change quickly, so frequent monitoring is necessary.

In simple terms, think of this balance as largely dominated by exports and imports. If the country consistently exports more than it imports, it usually runs a current account surplus. If it imports more than it exports, the current account swings into deficit. Viewed in isolation, when imports exceed exports locals sell their own currency to buy foreign currency to pay for the goods coming from abroad. As a currency is sold more than it is bought, it loses value. Now, if a country can also bring in enough foreign investment (i.e., foreigners bringing in foreign currency, selling it and buying domestic currency) then the depreciation effect might not happen.

So any executive should monitor the current account balance of countries in which they operate on a regular basis. Some international benchmarks say that the current account deficit should not exceed 3 or 4% of GDP for too long – if it does, this could lead to consistent, or worse, sudden depreciations. The trick is to check if the current account deficit is actually offset by enough foreign direct investment. If yes, that is good news and the risk of depreciation is reduced.

However, if the current account gap is not covered by healthy foreign direct investment but instead "hot money" inflows, executives should be aware that the currency might be strong for the wrong reasons; if the "hot money" leaves, the currency will suddenly fall. Also, if the current account gap is not covered by healthy foreign direct investment and "hot money" is also absent, the authorities probably need to spend their reserves or borrow to protect the value of their currency, and this might not be sustainable.

EPILOGUE

WE ARE CLEARLY MOVING into an exciting and exceptionally challenging period for executives operating in emerging markets. Pressures on executives to deliver more from emerging markets will increase and only those firms who take emerging markets seriously in terms of strategy, resources, focus and commitment, will do well. Anyone taking a half-hearted, short-termist approach will not manage to outperform the competition and won't achieve the desired sustainability.

As I wait to fly to the United States to brief the board of one of my multinational clients, I am thinking about the materials they sent me over to read. It shows they are market leaders in the US and most of Western Europe and have a presence in over a hundred emerging markets, but no market leadership in 85% if the emerging markets they operate in. In some places they are not even among the top five players. As I go through the documents, I can see why. And I am curious to know if the CEO, who I will meet for the first time, will want to commit to emerging markets in the long term, or if he is just a short-term, quarterly kind of guy. If he is a short-term guy, all the advice in this book will fall on deaf ears. As ever, meetings like that are just pure intellectual fun, regardless of the CEO's final decision!

Good luck to all of you trying to find more growth in these exciting markets – and safe travels!

BIBLIOGRAPHY

This book is almost exclusively based on the latest observations of corporate activity and conversations with senior corporate executives. However, in the background it partly relied on the following:

Kindleberger, Charles. *Manias, Panics and Crashes: A History of Financial Crisis*. Wiley Investment Classics, 2000.

Reinhart, C.M. and Rogoff K. *This Time is Different: Eight Centuries of Financial Folly*. Princeton University Press, 2011.

Papers on Asian crises and capital controls by Dani Rodrik.

Bagwhati, Jagdish. *In Defense of Globalization*. Oxford University Press, 2007.

Pacek, Nenad and Thorniley, Daniel. *Emerging Markets: Lessons for Business Success and Outlook for Different Markets* (2nd ed). Bloomberg Press, 2007.

Thought leadership and economic papers on various regions, countries and business issues by Global Success Advisors GmbH.

Russia business and economic papers by DT-Global Business Consulting GmbH.

Santiso, Javier. *Latin America's Political Economy of the Possible: Beyond Good Revolutionaries and Free-Marketeers.* The MIT Press, 2007.

Central banks and statistical offices of various countries

SOURCES FOR HR CHAPTER

Chartered Institute of Personnel & Development (CIPD, London) report on "Talent Development in the BRIC countries," January 2010.

Financial Times, 7 March 2012, pages 16 and 18

Reichheld, Frederick F. & Teal, Thomas, Bain & Co., *The Loyalty Effect*. Harvard Business School Press, 1996.

Investopedia.com: http://www.investopedia.com/terms/r/randd.asp#axzz1qGOgVDGz

JRC European Commission & Institute for Prospective, Technological Studies – "The 2010 EU industrial R&D investment scoreboard" – joint research center, European Commission, Hector Hernandez

"Developing Tomorrow's Leaders" (excerpt) by Kevin Dalton in *EFMD Global Focus*, Volume 05, Issue 03 2011

PWC – 14th annual CEO survey – 2011 – pwc.com

HR Connect Asia Pacific Comparative Employment Risks. AON Hewitt quoting US Department of Labor (http://www.aon.com/thought-leadership/asia-connect/2011-mar/understanding-people-risks-in-bric-part2.jsp#2)

Ingegerd Carlsson, Peter E. Wendt, Jarl Risberg: On the neurobiology of creativity. Differences in frontal activity between high and low creative subjects. Published in *Neuropsychologia 38* (2000) 873-885

Härén, Fredrik. *The Idea Book*. Interesting.org, 2006

Proctor, Tony. *Creative Problem Solving for Managers: Developing Skills for Decision-Making and Innovation*. Routledge, 2010.

Ray Michael L. and Myers, Rochelle. *Creativity in Business*. Broadway Books, NY, 1999.

ABOUT THE AUTHOR

NENAD PACEK and his businesses currently advise global and regional directors of almost 300 multinational corporations. He is founder and president of Global Success Advisors (global business and economic advisory) and co-founder of the CEEMEA Business Group corporate service (advisory for regional executives running Central Eastern Europe, Middle East and Africa). The advisory focus is on helping executives understand economic/business outlooks for virtually all countries around the world and on helping companies build strategies for sustainable growth in emerging markets.

Nenad is also author of *The Global Economy* (2012), lead author of *Emerging Markets: Lessons for Business Success and Outlook for Different Markets* (2003, 2007), and a contributor to the book *The Future of Money* (2010). He is one of the world's leading authorities on economic and business issues that concern multinational corporations seeking faster growth internationally. He performs on average two speeches every week at various corporate meetings on issues ranging from global, regional and country level economic/business outlooks to best business practices for outperforming competition internationally. In corporate circles he is well-known for not using any notes or power point slides while speaking and engaging in discussion.

Nenad is former Vice President of The Economist Group (Economist Intelligence Unit) where he spent almost two decades advising multinationals on economic and business issues and managing several business units in Europe, Middle East and Africa and one business unit globally. He chaired over 100 Economist Government Roundtables with Prime Ministers/Presidents and their cabinets throughout Western Europe, Eastern Europe, Middle East, Africa and Latin America.

Nenad is a board member of the Center for Creative Leadership (no. 1 provider of leadership education). He is guest faculty at Duke Corporate Education (no. 1 provider of corporate education), Notre Dame Executive MBA and a number of corporate universities.

Nenad grew up outside of the developed world, but was educated in Austria where he studied international business, finance and economics. He lives with his wife and (soon) three daughters near Vienna, Austria. He spends his rare free time mostly with his family, but occasionally sneaks out to play basketball, tennis, golf and to ski and swim.

For speeches and advisory sessions please contact Nenad Pacek directly at: nenad.pacek@globalsuccessadvisors.eu

See www.globalsuccessadvisors.eu for full biography, client testimonials and services.

See www.ceemeabusinessgroup.com for upcoming schedule of peer group meetings with Central Eastern Europe, Middle East and Africa (CEEMEA) Regional Directors in various European locations and Dubai, as well as upcoming schedule of economic/business updates on CEE/MEA markets.

BIOGRAPHIES OF CONTRIBUTORS TO THE HUMAN RESOURCES CHAPTER

SANJA HAAS is a former Procter and Gamble executive who consults and trains large global companies in the area of organizational strategy and leadership development. She is Senior Fellow and Human Capital Council Coordinator of The Conference Board in Brussels where she supports the Human Capital practice and is the Council's director for Learning, Leadership and Organizational Development. She lives in Brussels with her husband and two daughters.

Sanja Haas can be contacted at the following email: sanja@haasconsulting-co.net

ANTONIJA PACEK is a University of Cambridge-educated industrial psychologist. She currently helps companies improve their innovation potential through creativity assessment and training. Antonija co-developed CIP Survey®, a scientifically valid and holistic tool that measures creativity of both individuals and organizations. She previously worked with Hewitt Associates and the Center for Creative Leadership. She is a professor of Psychology at several universities in Vienna. In her free time she composes solo piano music and has published two albums. She lives near Vienna with her husband and (soon) three daughters.

Antonija Pacek can be contacted at the following email: antonija.pacek@globalsuccessadvisors.eu